THE PROBLEM OF
POPULATION

THE PROBLEM OF POPULATION

MORAL AND THEOLOGICAL CONSIDERATIONS

Introduced by

GEORGE N. SHUSTER

Edited by

DONALD N. BARRETT

Co-sponsored by

THE CANA CONFERENCE OF CHICAGO

UNIVERSITY OF NOTRE DAME PRESS · 1964

©
University of Notre Dame Press
1964

Library of Congress Catalog Card Number—64-17068

NOTRE DAME POCKET LIBRARY

— 3 —

PREFATORY NOTE

DONALD N. BARRETT

Minutes of the discussion were kept by Professor Donald Barrett except during one lengthy afternoon when a verbatim transcript was made. This transcript is referred to here as "the Jacobson notes." Naturally, an "integrated outline" will hardly reflect the vigorous give-and-take which characterized the sessions, many of which were informal and lasted far into the night. But it will provide in brief form a record of the major issues discussed and of the positions taken concerning them.

Those who participated in the Conference were Professor Donald N. Barrett, Department of Sociology, University of Notre Dame; Mr. Thomas K. Burch, Director of Demographic Studies for Population Research, Georgetown University; Reverend Kieran Conley, O.S.B., St. Meinrad Archabbey; Reverend Raymond F. Cour, C.S.C., Department of Political Science, University of Notre Dame; Professor Frederick J. Crosson, Department of Philosophy, University of Notre Dame; Reverend Francis Canavan, S.J., Associate Editor, *America*; Dr. William V. D'Antonio,

Department of Sociology, University of Notre Dame;
Professor John E. Dunsford, School of Law, St. Louis
University; Reverend Andrew Greeley, National
Opinion Research Center, University of Chicago;
Reverend George G. Hagmaier, C.S.P., Paulist Center
for Research, New York; Reverend Bernard Häring,
C.Ss.R., Rome, Italy; Reverend Raban Hathorn, O.S.B.,
St. Meinrad Archabbey; Reverend Walter Imbiorski,
The Cana Conference, Chicago; Reverend Robert O.
Johann, S.J., Loyola Seminary, Shrub Oak, New York;
Dr. John J. Kane, Department of Sociology, University
of Notre Dame; Reverend William Kenealy, S.J., Bos-
ton College Law School; Reverend Joseph Kerns, S.J.,
Wheeling College, Wheeling, West Virginia; Dr. Dud-
ley Kirk, Director, Demographic Division, The Popu-
lation Council, New York; Right Reverend Monsignor
J. C. Knott, National Catholic Welfare Conference;
Reverend Stanley Kutz, C.S.B., St. Michael's College,
Toronto, Canada; Reverend John Lynch, S.J., Weston
College, Weston, Massachusetts; Reverend Richard
McCormick, S.J., West Baden University, West Baden
Springs, Indiana; Reverend Thomas McDonough,
Calvert House, University of Chicago; Reverend John
A. O'Brien, University of Notre Dame; Mr. James
O'Gara, Managing Editor, *Commonweal*; Reverend M.
O'Leary, Catholic Marriage Advisory Council, Lon-
don, England; Reverend John J. O'Sullivan, St. Paul
Seminary, St. Paul, Minnesota; Reverend John Reedy,
C.S.C., Editor, *Ave Maria*; Reverened Thomas J.
Reese, Catholic Welfare Guild; Reverend Henry J.
Sattler, Family Life Bureau, N.C.W.C.; Mr. Philip

Scharper, Editor, Sheed & Ward, Inc.; Dr. George N. Shuster, Assistant to the President, University of Notre Dame; and Reverend John L. Thomas, St. Louis University.

The Conference opened on September 5, 1963, and closed on September 8, 1963.

CONTENTS

x   Contents

Introduction

GEORGE N. SHUSTER

This book contains the papers written by a group of distinguished Catholic scholars brought together at Notre Dame to consider one of the most difficult and crucial problems with which society must now wrestle. In its most dramatic form, the problem is that of increasing population. But it is much broader in scope. What is the family in this our time? What is the right ordering of the relationship between the man and the woman who agree in marriage to create a loving union? How shall we think of the responsibilities to be assumed for children brought into the world? Finally devout Christians and Jews will ask a still more fundamental question: what is the obligation of human love to Divine love? If God's will is to be done on earth, how shall we discern and interpret His will in so far as marriage and the family are concerned?

No one of these queries is easy to answer. Some are new, or at least have not been put into the context of modern industrial and technological society. They are profoundly troubling questions, and those who ask

them often virtually despair of finding the right solutions. As this book will indicate, theologians who
considered them were in former years far too often
likely to present abstractions which few of those who
read or listened could relate effectively to the situations in which they found themselves. In short, here,
as in other areas, the lack of effective thought was all
too manifest. Small wonder, then, that the non-
Catholic public could generally discover no clue to
what it was which dictated alleged Catholic doctrine
on a matter of such grave importance. Barriers were
erected which were far less the products of divergent
moral conviction than they were fences built by
language. Nor could it be avowed that Catholics themselves understood. For if they had they would have
been able to explain their position more effectively.

It is for this reason that Notre Dame University began
to consider some months ago what its contribution to
the study and discussion of Problems of Population
might be. After an initial conference of exploration,
which brought many distinguished demographers to
the campus for informal talks, two of those in attend-
ance expressed the hope that there might be arranged
further conferences to discuss questions about which
there needed to be established as much of a Catholic
consensus as could be attained. These two were the
Reverend Walter Imbiorski and the Reverend John L.
Thomas, S.J. In constant cooperation with them, Notre
Dame invited those whose papers are reprinted in this
book to address a Conference held during September
1963. Membership in the Conference was by invita-

tion. Unfortunately some persons we would have liked to have with us were not free to come; and even more regrettably not all who wished to attend could be accommodated. Even so the group was unusual not merely because of the level of competence but also because of their candor and their willingness to spend long hours in discussion. The names of all are given in the Prefatory Note.

As will be apparent, this book is largely devoted to clarifying the teaching of the Catholic Church. We asked ourselves this question: what is at issue when the Problem of Population is discussed, and what can we reliably say is the Catholic view? The reader will soon discover for himself that those who addressed themselves to it are not propagandists but earnest students who seek clarity for themselves and others. No attempt is made to explain away either the difficulties or the advantages inherent in the Catholic position. It is of course true that if the group had been differently constituted we might well have obtained another product. Accordingly, a word should doubtless be said here about how the selection was made. First we took for granted a fairly obvious fact, namely that Jesuit scholars were those who had devoted most time to the study of the problem; and so three of the papers were written by Jesuits. We also chose one of Notre Dame's most capable philosophers and a member of St. Louis University's Faculty of Law. Although Father Häring could not be with us during the Conference, he spent a day at Notre Dame during the course of which the interview here reprinted was completed and edited.

We consider ourselves fortunate in having been able to present this document to our Conference so that it could be thoroughly discussed.

We are grateful to the Ford Foundation for the grant which made this Conference possible. It is to be followed by two others, the next of which will explore the problem in terms of Welfare and Charity agencies. We are likewise deeply appreciative of the fact that the Cana Conference of Chicago co-sponsored our endeavor, and that His Eminence, Albert Cardinal Meyer, gave it his blessing in advance. This last fact suffices to indicate that Catholic inquiry in this area is both needed and reputable.

Christian Marriage and Family Planning

FATHER JOHN A. O'BRIEN INTERVIEWS
FATHER BERNARD HÄRING, C.Ss.R.

Father Häring, you are a peritus *at the Council and also a consultor for the theological commission of the Council. Hence you are familiar with the thought of this commission on the subject of marriage. Would you give us a little insight into the thinking of the theological commission on marriage?*

ANSWER: I would not dare to speak here in the name of the theological commission, but let me express what I see to be the whole attitute of the Second Vatican Council. It is a very positive, constructive, pastoral approach to the crucial questions which face married people in the modern world. A pastoral approach does not mean withdrawing or denying any moral doctrinal principle, but it means a better integration, a better synthesis, a positive acknowledgment of the values of conjugal love and a more careful distinction between different attitudes.

First, I do not think it is possible to give a pastoral response to these problems by overemphasizing the conjugal act itself and its biological performance. The first consideration must be given to responsible parenthood.

QUESTION: *Do you think that in this field of responsible parenthood we can meet with all the other Christians and even non-Christians?*

ANSWER: To a great extent we can use a common psychological approach. It is only a very small group of people who still think that children should be taken as they come, without any reflection. At least in European and American culture the great majority of people, Catholics as well as non-Catholics, are convinced that procreation is essentially a question of responsibility.

A husband who makes his wife pregnant in spite of a clear diagnosis that this would endanger her life is, in the common opinion, judged as a man without a sense of responsibility and love, a man sinning against justice. It is of great importance to purify the concept of responsible parenthood. Birth control and family planning meant from the beginning, and still today often mean, a human reckoning without consideration of eternal values. At least some representatives of planned parenthood mean this—the highest value is to keep up the present standard of living, especially of the upper social classes and of the privileged nations.

They mean that people can once and for all make the decision that they will have so many, for instance, one or two children, and no more. Responsible parenthood in view of Catholic morality means giving a generous response to the challenging appeal of the gifts of God. Nobody can make this act of judgment as to what responsibility means for them other than married couples themselves, in consideration of all the factors of their lives, especially health, home conditions and educational facilities.

QUESTION: *What decision, Father Häring, must a married couple make?*

ANSWER: They must make the decision as to whether another child is desirable *now.* They do not make a judgment once and forever. They make it only for the present time and remain open to the challenge of a new situation. Responsible parenthood can be expressed in the basic principle of Christian morality, "What can I return to God for all that He has given me?"

In the light of this principle, responsible parenthood can mean for one family not to desire more than one child. It can mean for another to desire, even after the tenth child, one more. The judgment of responsibility is necessarily also an authentic image of the religious and moral life of those who make it. There is here also an essential growth of generosity, which cannot be imposed from without by any human authority. Only if married people are growing in the whole of sanctity can they be expected to be absolutely generous in this regard. It would be a great error and a contradiction of the whole concept of Christian morality if we were to impose roughly upon all high heroism in this area without respect to the law of growth and without preparation for this heroism in the whole of Christian life.

QUESTION: *As you know, Father Häring, we are confronted with the challenge of a population explosion unprecedented in human history. This demands that*

*we face in a realistic, down-to-earth manner the need
of adapting the mores of procreation and stressing the
need of family planning, and hence the enormous
responsibility of parenthood today. Would you com-
ment upon the way of meeting the challenge of an
exploding population?*

ANSWER: I do not think that the population explosion
has a shocking aspect only for North America but also
for the whole world. In particular those nations which
have a greater responsibility for the world of today
are faced with this problem. It is not only the population explosion as a social problem and a world problem
which nations and married couples have to face, but
also the problem of responsible parenthood and the
means of carrying it out in almost every family. Moral
and pastoral theology have to consider the sociological,
cultural and economic background of principles
formed in earlier times, and they must be reconsidered
in view of the present situation.

QUESTION: *Father Häring, do you think that a reconsideration of the Catholic doctrine on planned parenthood and contraception is theologically possible?*

ANSWER: I think, and surely many share my opinion,
that moral theology and the official doctrines of the
Church show a great progress in rethinking and reformulating these problems. The famous historical
question of usury is a typical example of how economic and sociological changes oblige the Church to
rethink some moral conclusions and formulate new
principles.

In former ages the Church forbade absolutely the

taking of interest on capital. The *Council of Vienne* (1311-1312) declared in a decree (not in a doctrinal constitution): "If one would fall into the error to assert that one could lend money for interest without sinning, then it is our decision that he has to be treated as a heretic, and we give the order to the bishops and to the inquisitors to proceed with the greatest severity against those who are suspected of having fallen into this error."[1]

It was long before Pope Pius XI in the encyclical, *Quadragesimo Anno*, stressed the right to interest on capital. How can we explain such a change which seems to be a direct contradiction on a doctrinal question? Only a clear insight into the great difference between the economic structure of earlier times and that of our modern industrialized society can explain the reconsideration and reformulation of the doctrine of the Church in this matter.

In earlier times capital was not fruitful and was loaned only to those who were in distress. To demand interest from them would have been the same as to misuse the need of a neighbor for the selfish enrichment of those who were in better economic situations. In our modern times capital is generally loaned to those who use it for their own economic interest.

Capital in a dynamic economy is by its nature, or, rather by the whole of the economic structure, fruitful. While it is justifiable to demand a moderate rate of interest from those to whom one loans his capital, it

[1] *Decreta* N. 29, *Conciliorum Decumenicorum Decreta* (Romanae Triburgi, 1962), p. 360 f.

remains still true that nobody is allowed to misuse the painful situation of the poor for his own profit. Christians still know that it is a great work of social charity to lend money without interest if that is the way to save a man or his family from misery.

QUESTION: *Father Häring, do you think that the problem of responsible parenthood is similar to that of usury?*

ANSWER: My answer to a great extent would be Yes. In earlier times children were an essential goal for the economic and social needs of the family. The assurance for old age and the function of the family as a unit of production made it desirable to have many children. Furthermore, there was no medical diagnosis as to the dangers of a new pregnancy. Infant mortality was generally more than 50 or 60 per cent. The problems of education in a static society were not too complicated. All this has changed. In many cases it would be catastrophic for a young family to have four children in the first four years. The health of the mother would be totally exhausted, the financial situation desperate, and so on. Not a lack of generosity but rather a sense of responsibility and realism imposes on the young couple the necessity of spacing pregnancies from the very beginning. This is necessary even if they wish a large family under good conditions.

QUESTION: *Father, would you speak briefly concerning the usefulness for theologians of sociological research in the field of marriage?*

ANSWER: There is no doubt that sociological research in this field is not only useful but also necessary for theologians. In a static or only slightly changing world a theologian could merely re-echo the conclusions and even the very formulations of the last generation. In our day, we must apply to this area the scriptural concept to be watchful and to recognize the signs of the times.

If we do not use all legitimate means of psychological and sociological research, we cannot speak to men of today. We will not be heard nor will we be understood. I think that our Natural Law arguments against contraception are not understood or accepted by the majority because of this lack of necessary study of the sociological, economic, cultural situation, and the psychological and moral attitude of the people of today.

Socio-psychological research can show us that married people of today consider the problems of marriage fundamentally in terms of conjugal love, and they consider the Natural Law arguments, neglecting the reality of married love and relegating it to a secondary and nonessential place, as unrealistic and even immoral.

QUESTION: *But, Father Häring, is it not an unchangeable principle of Catholic doctrine that procreation and education of offspring are the primary ends of marriage and married love only a secondary end?*

ANSWER: I think that in this question we touch the most crucial aspect of the failure of many of our manuals and pastoral methods. Often Canon Law was considered the final response to the marriage problems of the day, and the exposition of Canon Law that mutual help (*mutuum adjutorium*) is only a secondary end was misunderstood. Mutual help is only one of the expressions of conjugal love and surely a secondary end in comparison with the procreation and education of children. However, conjugal love is infinitely more than mutual help.

Among theologians it is more and more becoming a common conviction that married love is first to be considered not as a goal or end of the marriage but as the *causa formalis*, the very essence of the marriage as a sacrament and the image and likeness of the covenant of love between Christ and the Church. If everything is in order, the betrothed couple go to the nuptials not because they are to have children but because they *want* to have children.

Also if everything is in order, the betrothed couple go to the altar because they already love one another and promise, therefore, love and fidelity "until death do us part." They do not say, "We wish to be married that later on we may love one another." This simple phenomenology shows us that love and procreation run in the same order of causality.

QUESTION: *What, Father Häring, do you consider to be the primary end of marriage?*

ANSWER: Procreation is the *causa finalis* or the primary end or, as Cardinal Suenens says, it is the most specifying end of marriage and of married love. I insist, however, that procreation and the education of offspring are not, actually, the end of a mere contract. They are the inborn and most essential end of the very covenant of love, and the contract must be seen in this light. They are a *yes* to the unity and indissolubility of a love which is ordained to the service of life.

This explanation surely does not diminish the dignity and importance of the service of life but shows its strongest and most wonderful foundation. It is one of the most dangerous errors against psychological reality and the very essence of the sacrament of marriage to consider married love something like a dangerous competition with procreation and education.

Married love is the most basic condition for the right service of love and for the right procreation and education of the children. Married love is a source of parental love. Both the encounter with modern psychological attitudes and the development of the doctrine of spirituality of marriage demand a doctrinal and pastoral approach which emphasizes the high importance of conjugal love and the necessity of cultivating married love.

QUESTION: *Do you think, Father Häring, that these doctrinal considerations have an impact upon the ways and means of responsible parenthood? Could these considerations make unavoidable a change in our moral convictions or at least in our pastoral methods?*

ANSWER: The answer to this urgent question is not easy. They should not be considered as making for an easier moral code. Therefore my first answer would be: these considerations constitute a nobler and stronger challenge to married people to watch over the purity and vitality of their love in the conjugal act as well as in the whole of the married and domestic life.

As to the sexual life, it is evident that this integration

from the viewpoint of love means a redeemed and re-
deeming love, and therefore a continuous effort of
purification and growth in such a love. A Natural Law
consideration which places the accent only on a right
biological performance of the conjugal act remains on
the level of mere animals and considers as primary
what man has in common with the animals.

It forgets the higher needs of the persons and therefore necessarily remains a very poor minimalism.
Often and almost unavoidably it leads to a very rigid
attitude in this narrow area. The first and noblest
obligation in married life is an unselfish giving of oneself and a grateful acceptance of the giving of the
other. The success of married life as well as the readiness to the service of life depends on the constant
cultivation of this attitude of true and genuine love.
The essential question of conscience of the married
couple is: Are we at least honestly and sincerely striving towards this ideal?

A consideration of married life which takes into account chiefly the biological factor neglects not only the
natural importance of married love and the very essence of the sacrament as a supernatural covenant of
love, but also the actual needs arising from the changed
psychological and sociological context. The rigorism
which forbids almost all tenderness to those couples
who do not and should not wish a new pregnancy is
responsible for many broken homes and broken
hearts.

If the first preoccupation is not to lose the seed in contact or in the nearness of the husband and wife, then

a thousand other dangers arise. The husband, and in many cases also the wife, is working outside the home in continuous contact with persons of the opposite sex. If they do not continuously cultivate conjugal love (not merely a platonic general love), they will feel the sexual appeal and fascination of others. Furthermore, they lose in many cases the openness to procreative love in their own marriage.

As we pointed out in the answer to an earlier question, the spacing of pregnancies can have a very positive and constructive meaning in the context of real generosity. It can also be the expression of intimate tenderness and the becoming of one flesh in conjugal intercourse during those times in which a new pregnancy is not desirable.

QUESTION: *Does not* Casti Connubii *judge as guilty of grievous sin those couples who perform a conjugal act frustrating the purpose of procreation?*

ANSWER: Here we are on the crucial question of how to apply the text of Genesis 38:9-10 to the problems and difficulties of married people of our time. Can those generous couples who wish to have the maximum number of children they can honestly and properly bring up be charged like Onan who betrayed Thamar, the widow of his brother and his whole kinship by denying her any right of a child and by desiring the property of his brother as his own?

There is no doubt that the basic principle of *Casti Connubii*, "What is essentially against nature can never and for no reason be justified as morally good," remains intact. However, the use of the biblical argument (Genesis 38:9f) in *Casti Connubii* does not prove what it wished to prove. The situation and the intention of married couples who have good and sometimes absolutely obligating reasons not to desire a pregnancy are totally different from the situation of Onan, who was killed by God because of the betrayal of his wife and of his kinship.

If the principle of responsible parenthood is accepted (and as you, Father O'Brien, showed in your articles in *Ave Maria, Look* and *Today's Family* it is generally accepted in the actual teaching of the Church), if this principle is valid and if the couple has made its judgment in full sincerity, the biological fact of the loss of the seed cannot be considered a direct sin against the primary end of the marriage. A Natural Law consideration which compares these good couples with Onan, the brutal sinner of Genesis 38, makes unbelievable the whole of the marriage doctrine of Catholic moralists not only to Protestants and Jews but also to our best Catholic lay people.

Sometimes people have the impression that *natural* means only *biological* and the primary goal means what man has in common with animals. It is the primary goal of marriage which makes necessary the cultivation of conjugal love and tenderness at those times in which a new pregnancy would hurt the sense of responsibility of the couple. This cultivation of love must keep alive the source of the service of life and must preserve that unity of the parents in one flesh which creates the best conditions for unity and charity in the education of the children.

If it is true that some married people do not need this

because of an extraordinarily high spirituality and because they have permeated a thousand other expressions of life with their conjugal love, it still remains true that many and perhaps the greatest majority need these expressions of tenderness and also, at least from time to time, the becoming of one flesh in the fullest sense. The deliberate abuse of conjugal intercourse by those who could and should wish the first child or a larger family has quite a different moral meaning than the deficiencies and weaknesses of those married people who, at the present time, can and should not wish a new pregnancy.

Sometimes our Natural Law arguments are expressed in terms of a time in which every conjugal intercourse was judged only from the one goal of procreation. As to Genesis 38, Father A.-M. Debarle, O.P., has proved in a splendid study[2] that before St. Augustine none of the Fathers of the Church had applied it to the difficulties of married people or specifically to contraception.

As Father Debarle clearly shows, St. Augustine never did so in his sermons but only in his writings. His arguments to a great extent lose their value, for he asserts that every conjugal intercourse is sinful if the couple does not actually have the intention of procreating a new life. As this basic opinion of St. Augustine is, at least since the time of St. Alphonsus, generally rejected by Catholic moralists, the whole of his thought must be reconsidered in a new context.

QUESTION: *Father Häring, could consequently some*

[2] "La Bible et les Pères ont-ils parlés de la contraception," in *Supplement de la vie Spirituelle* 1962, 573-610.

means of contraception besides the already approved rhythm method be considered as not sinful or at least not gravely sinful?

ANSWER: This does not necessarily follow. In the discussion we must distinguish the person, and the *opus personae*, from the mere function of nature, the *opus naturae*. My personal conviction is that the use of condom and diaphragm modify the personal act and almost invariably mislead the expression of conjugal love into selfishness. They hinder what the Bible calls a mutual knowing of oneself. But it must at least be considered that some married couples assert, with full sincerity, that they made progress in an unselfish love for one another more when they used this means than in times of total abstinence and the consequent hypertension.[3]

Furthermore, we must consider the possibility of the invincible ignorance of many good-minded people. One of the reasons is a strong public opinion and the other, the unintegrated Natural Law teaching of some of our moralists or priests. Neither would I try to justify the method of withdrawal. I say method because if it is a method it is a deliberate tension to the moment of the orgasm, and this spoils the personal

---

[3] Generally the couple who use this only because of a special circumstance recognize that it hurts their own dignity and respectful love, and they give it up as soon as the worst distress has passed. Today, even the apostles of planned parenthood acknowledge that the appliance methods (especially the use of the condom) are disagreeable and that the Enovid or the Anovlar steroids are more in keeping with the aesthetic feeling and dignity of the persons involved.

act of giving oneself and in achieving the full unity in one flesh.

From this method of withdrawal is totally distinct the action of those married people who really intended self-control and a respectful expression of intimate tenderness, even if by chance an orgasm happens at least from time to time. I think we can go a step further. What *Casti Connubii* brands as mortal sin is the deliberate and free withdrawal.

If married people who are convinced that they should not have a new pregnancy go too far in the expression of tenderness and, without previous deliberate intention, begin the union, and then in the moment of awakening withdraw, this cannot be considered as a *method* of withdrawal or, as such, a *deliberate act*. In many cases married couples would have good reason to doubt, at least, that this would be a mortal sin. From the viewpoint of their own actual conscience it can be an imperfection, a venial sin or a dangerous lack of self-control. The important question remains how sincerely they are striving towards a greater purity of conjugal love and a motivated control of self.

QUESTION: *Father, are all sins against the Sixth Commandment considered mortal sins?*

ANSWER: It is surely the doctrine of the Church that chastity is a high virtue and a very important expression of what is true and genuine love for God and neighbor. Therefore, it is a grave obligation of every man, and especially of Christians, to strive towards full chastity in accordance with his state of life. It is to be considered a mortal sin if one, knowing the needs of the virtue of charity, deliberately and with full freedom acts in the opposite way.

In a dynamic expression it would mean also that one puts himself in the most extreme danger if he does not strive towards the deep respect for the mystery of marriage and sexuality and towards the self-control which safeguards the expression of this respect. But the lack of striving can have very different degrees. There can be merely imperfection, conscious venial sin or mortal sin.

The traditional moral theology does not consider every indirect sin against chastity a mortal sin. That means that if a man exposes himself to danger against chastity, in most cases there is not a full deliberation and a full free will, nor a clear insight as to how great these dangers are or how far the obligation extends to avoid them.

Generally speaking, the Sixth Commandment is not to be considered under different principles than the other great virtues and commandments. Nobody can doubt that the commandment of love of one's neighbor (as Christ loved us) is the greatest of all commandments. Nevertheless, not all signs against fraternal charity are mortal sins. God takes absolutely seriously all His commandments, but He knows our human weaknesses.

The last and final possibility and reality of venial sin comes from human weakness and consequently from the imperfection of the human act. Furthermore, the whole Christian life, and especially the virtue of chastity in matrimony and outside of matrimony, demands from all children of Adam at times a long, energetic, and patient striving.

We should not consider as mortal sinners couples who are generous in their judgment as to responsible parenthood, who are living in real charity and generosity and praying for perseverance; we should not consider them as mortal sinners if, in spite of good will, they do not yet understand all the needs of a full conjugal chastity and if they do not even obtain the perfect performance of what they understand as a need of the virtue of conjugal chastity. Here we could remember the wonderful words of St. Augustine, speaking on the man who had fallen into the hands of the robbers and whom the merciful Samaritan brought into the inn:

Non ita potest ad iustitiae culmen ascendere sicut potuit inde descendere, qui etiam si iam stabulo est, adhuc curatur. Non igitur Deus impossibilia iubet; sed iubendo admonet, et facere quod passis, et petere quod non passis.[4]

[A man cannot so quickly reach the heights of justice as when he has fallen down from it. Even though he is already in the Church (in the inn of redemption), he still needs help. In this sense it is understood that God does not demand impossible things from us. By demanding, God admonishes us to do what we can do and to pray sincerely to obtain what we cannot yet do.]

In the context it is evident that according to St. Augustine, it can be necessary to pray a long time until man has reached the full height of virtue.

I do not think that the doctrine of the Catholic Church

[4] *De Natura et Gratia*, c. 42, *PL* 44, 271.

on married life will be changed in basic principles, but the whole of this doctrine can be better integrated into the great commandment of love and into the fundamental law of growth. It must be presented in a dynamic approach. That means in a pastoral approach which shows in joyous faith, the height, the depth, the length and the breadth of a life in Christ Jesus, but an approach also which shows how to take the next step and to prepare the way for the second and the third step.

QUESTION: *What do you think of Dr. Rock's pill, Enovid?*

ANSWER: There is a statement of Pope Pius XII, one of the last utterances immediately before his death, an utterance which gives a clear outline of some principles and leaves other questions open. The final decision of the Church as to these problems has not yet been given. Many European theologians and at least several American moralists think that the opinion which will probably be given is that the use of these pills at the time of lactation is permissible, even if the mother is not capable of nursing her child. The reasons are the following. It seems very probable that there is at least a trend of nature to prevent ovulation, and consequently a new pregnancy, at the time of actual lactation.

This is statistically proved to be still true in the majority of cases but there is not sufficient certainty. As civilization and the whole economic and social changes have, to some extent, interfered with the nature and function of sexual life, there must be a possibility of a deliberate interference with them, an interference which establishes their lost balance. Thus it is so in the very direction of nature itself.

Among Catholic gynecologists there are other discussions about the principle of the lesser evil. An operation is always an evil. It is an interference into the work of nature, and it is a moral evil if the interference is arbitrary. In analogy this *arbitrary* interference with ovulation (that is, with the functioning of the nature of the woman) is always bad. But if there is a great moral probability of certainty that rhythm does not suffice and that a full expression of conjugal love is almost necessary for a normal married life and even for the unity of the family, then such interference with the functioning of nature by progesterone cannot be considered in every case as arbitrary.

Then there are discussions to to whether such intervention in very difficult cases must be considered as a lesser evil in a moral sense or only in a physical sense. In a moral sense this would mean: It is still objectively sinful, but this could be considered as a way out of deeper moral misery into the full light. If followed by those who consider it morally right, we could apply the great principle of Cardinal Newman, "Whoever follows sincerely his conscience, even if the conscience is erroneous, is on the way into the full light" (of truth and virtue). Other gynecologists and some moralists[5] go much farther and consider this as only a lesser evil in a physical sense.

[5] Generally, they are much more advanced in their personal convictions than in publications. This is without doubt a very

It is considered as a nondangerous biological interference which makes possible the full and correct
personal encounter in the marital act. But everyone
would insist that such an interference would be bad
if, in that certain case, it would be arbitrary—without
good and strong moral reasons.

At the present time we have great hopes that the new
pill Duphaston, produced by the Philip Roxane Company and approved by the Food and Drug Administration, can give an exact fixation and knowledge of the
days of ovulation. Then with an abstinence of a mere
four or five days, the rhythm method would have the
necessary certainty for all couples, and no couple of
good will could assert that these sacrifices are beyond
the human endurance of faithful Christians.

Duphaston does not suppress any function of nature,
but brings it to perfect performance and stability.
From the moral viewpoint we could hardly make any
objection to its use, but in the meantime it is still in
the experimental stage.

QUESTION: *Do you mean then, Father Häring, that
this pill will be conducive to the salvation of not a
few couples?*

ANSWER: I cannot believe that eternal salvation of
well-minded married people would depend upon the
good or bad function of a pill. We would be happy

serious problem. To some extent it is natural and necessary
that we all are more cautious when we appear in public than
when we discuss these problems only in small groups. This is a
sign of respectability and modesty, but it seems to me that the
difference between a large public opinion and the publications
of moralists is alarming.

if this pill would help to diminish difficulties and tensions, but the essential condition for salvation will always remain the genuine good will of the faithful to do what they can and to strive constantly towards better performance, praying for the grace to do that which they cannot yet perfectly achieve.

Our pastoral practice was at least to some extent contaminated by an all too material consideration of external *success*. The essence must be a great and deep respect for the full Christian ideal and an earnest striving, step by step, towards a better fulfillment.

QUESTION: *Father Häring, the subject that is today the occasion of great tension between Catholics and non-Catholics in this country, and probably in most of the civilized countries, is that of birth control. Non-Catholics in general, and an increasing number of lay Catholics as well, are completely unable to understand the cogency of the traditional Natural Law argument against contraception. It seems to be a mere play on words and practically the whole medical world as well as all non-Catholic churchmen regard the use of medically approved contraceptive methods as not only legitimate at times, but also at times morally necessary. Do you see the possibility of thinking through this question anew and of some significant changes in the light of new conditions in the world?*

ANSWER: Father O'Brien, I must express how much I appreciate your article in *Look*, "Let's Take Birth Control out of Politics," October 10, 1961. To the good and fundamental reasons you gave for taking this subject out of our political discussions, I would like to add one more. The history of the moral theology of the last fifteen centuries proves that there is a genuine development of doctrine, a possibility of a better integration, better arguments and some very necessary distinctions.

We Catholics of today do not think that we have resolved all problems in this area. We still have the tremendous task of expressing the principles of the Gospel in an understandable way to our faithful for the actual needs of our time. We can even profit by a friendly discussion of these problems with our non-Catholic or non-Christian neighbors.

We can learn from them some insights into physiology, psychology, sociology and anthropology. A sincere and respectful dialogue can be helpful to a deeper understanding and a better expression of the essential principles of the tradition of the Catholic Church. All these deliberations and discussions must reflect the ecumenical atmosphere of the Second Vatican Council.

Relevant Currents in the History of Sexuality

JOSEPH KERNS, S.J.

Now the Spirit expressly says that in later times men will depart from the faith, by giving heed to deceitful spirits and doctrines of diabolical origin, propagated through the dissembling of liars who have a seared conscience. They will forbid marriage and enjoin abstinence from foods. . . .[1]

This warning that St. Paul addresses to his young co-worker, Timothy, embodies the reason for this particular paper. The Church's words on marriage have usually been prompted by some practical problem, some actual historical situation. It might aid our discussion of her teachings if we turn our attention briefly to their historical context, so that we can notice what is perennial and what changes with every age, what is revealed by God and what is an accident of culture.

Less than a century after Paul's death it was apparent that he has been all too reliable a prophet. Ireneus, the bishop of Lyons in modern France, whose teachers had known the Apostles personally, relates how "Satu-

[1] I Tim. 4: 3.

rinus and Marcion, who are called 'the Continent,' preached that all should refrain from marriage. . . ."[2]

The Fathers of the Greek-speaking church during the late 300's kept attacking similar movements in sermons, essays, poems. And as Europe entered the Middle Ages, a new emergency was evident from the tone of the bishops who assembled at Arras in 1025. The old pagan gloom which saw matter as evil and marriage as a sin had begun to settle on one French town after another. These were the days of the Cathars, the Pure Ones.

Theologians of the new wave of learning that coursed through Europe during the 1100's found themselves compelled to refute assertions such as:

Husbands must abstain from relations with the women joined to them in legitimate marriage, and also from meat and milk, fish and wine for three years. . . .

Likewise, no layman will be saved, though he has found the road to every virtue, unless he becomes a monk.[3]

In 1215 the question was pondered by the bishops at the Fourth Lateran Council. With all the authority of an ecumenical council they declared, "Not only virgins and celibates but also married people who please God by right faith and good conduct merit to arrive at eternal happiness."[4]

But in 1307 the archbishop of Cologne listed among his charges against the Beghards: "They also say: 'Unless a woman grieves at the loss of her virginity in

[2] *Contra Haereses*, lib. 1, c. 28, *PG* 7, 690.
[3] Council of Constantinople, *Acta*, Mansi 21, 583.
[4] *De Fide Catholica*, c. 1, *DB 430*.

marriage and by her grief deplores the fact, she cannot be saved.' "[5]

As late as 1578 the Spanish Inquisition complained of the Alumbrados, "4. By their way of speaking they belittle the sacrament of Matrimony. . . ."[6]

Though symptoms of this rigorism continued to appear among groups like the Jansenists, they were no longer so pronounced. Bishops did not seem as alarmed as before, and the stream of formal condemnations gradually petered out.

But one fact which emerges from these centuries of struggle cannot be ignored if we would hope to see marriage as Christ has revealed it. Each of these sects was a product of the times. Its theology was as new and distinctive as the culture in which it appeared. And yet one doctrine is found among all of them: Marriage is evil.

This cannot be just a conclusion that happens to follow logically from a particular set of ideas. It is the expression of something deeper, a vague stubborn temperamental suspicion which takes different forms in different times and countries as it comes upon different general theories about God and man which seem to confirm it.

Whatever its origins, they are not Christian. Gnosticism is older than the Church. The Manichaeans took their rise in Persia. And yet this uneasiness about the

---

[5] Hartzheim, *Concilia Germaniae*, Vol. IV, 101ff. Cited by De Guibert, *Documenta Ecclesiastica Christianae Perfectionis Studium Spectantia,* Rome: P.U.G., 1931, p. 154.
[6] De Guibert, *op. cit.*, p. 228.

fact of being male and female is part of the climate in which the Church has lived for most of its history.

The presence of Christ at Cana should settle any doubts as to what God thinks of marriage. Around the year 400 both Greek and Latin Fathers took this for granted, and their teaching has been echoed down to the present day. The episode at Cana was symbolic. Like the Father in the Old Testament, so Christ in the New presents Himself as the founder of marriage. It cannot be opposed to religion. God is the one responsible for it. It enters into that awesome design by which His will for the human race is to be accomplished.

But how? As something He positively favors or as a concession He makes to human weakness? It was not long before the Church was forced to realize that this was not an academic question. A cultural uneasiness about marriage that was strong enough to make some leave the Church could not help but affect even those who remained. During the late 300's some of the Greek Fathers declared that marriage, though not sinful in itself, was the result of original sin. It was simply a means of preserving a race of creatures who now must die.

But despite the suspicion of these eminent Christians, it has always been the considered view of the Church that marriage is neither a sin nor the result of sin. Even if the first man and woman had lived an ideal life, one feature of that life would have been marriage.

Still, the very Christians who saw this from the beginning had suspicions of their own. In the writings of Augustine and others who copied him for a thou-

sand years we find, not marriage, but the sex instinct
traced to original sin. Sexual intercourse is permitted
between husband and wife only because the three
assets of marriage, offspring, fidelity, and the sacred
pledge, give it a distinctive quality which makes it
morally good. It is not good in itself, but only in this
setting. The sex instinct is an effect of original sin
and indelibly tainted by its origin. To allow such an
evil force to express itself would be to perpetuate the
primal rebellion. Sexual intercourse always needs an
excuse. The pleasure it involves may be tolerated but
never desired.

A significant fact about these norms of conduct was
alluded to by Augustine himself. There are Catholics
who find it easier not to marry than to live by them.
It seems more than a coincidence that all through the
centuries during which writers echo him there are also
continual assertions that marital relations in actual
practice always involve sin. The general—and some
said, universal—practice of Catholic couples was
evidently at variance with the moral principles that
flow from Augustine's analysis.

If we hope to discover how marriage has appeared to
those who have seen it in the light of Christ's revelation, this counter trend cannot be ignored. These married people were the Church. They were the majority
of its members. True, they were not official teachers.
Still, baptism gave them a genuine share of that insight
which is faith.

Then, too, though they had heard about Adam and
Eve, they were completely unaware of what profes-

sional theologians were writing about the sex instinct and original sin. Most of them could not read. Saxon villagers and recently converted Lombards knew little more of Augustine than his name. The liturgical cycle gave them a view of life. They lived by their general Catholic instinct and rarely felt the need of anything else. Without special thought on the matter, they married and then made use of their marriage rights.

And no one told them they were wrong. They cannot be compared with Catholics today who practice contraceptive birth control. Whatever be the reason, the fact remains that, from Augustine's time till the Middle Ages, their ordinary conduct may be lamented in books, but nothing is said to them directly. Adulterers are castigated from the pulpit. Neo-Manichaeans are condemned. But there are no sermons on this theme, no prayers in the liturgy. The whole discussion on the origin of the sex instinct took place among a relatively secluded group of professionals using Latin in an age that could not read.

And the way in which these scholars reacted to the situation merits attention. What they knew of Augustine's theology and what they knew of the married life of Catholics in their day seemed to converge on one conclusion: These couples were continually guilty of sin. As long as they merely read Augustine, this is what they concluded. But then they started their own investigation. By the 1100's certain precisions began to appear. Both theologians and canon lawyers agreed with a passing remark of Augustine that, even when there was no question of having children, one married person did not sin in acceding to the other's desire of intercourse when the latter would otherwise be tempted to seek satisfaction elsewhere. The demands of the sex instinct were satisfied in this case to avoid a greater evil.

But if one of the partners might thus avert this greater evil from the other, some writers began to surmise that he might do the same for himself. By the 1500's this was the accepted view. The theologians who held it did not ignore earlier writers, but neither were they afraid to rely on their own personal observation of life in the Church.

This is evident in a remark by Dominic Soto. Though he felt, along with medieval theologians, that intercourse is blameless only if the motive which prompts it is one of the aims of marriage, he adds: "It is not required that married people actually have these aims in mind when they come together. It is enough if there is a virtual relation, in other words, if they introduce no evil circumstance."[7]

They need not be thinking explicitly about one of the aims of marriage. Soto was not alone in this opinion. By 1602, when the treatise appeared which was to give Thomas Sanchez his reputation, it was apparent that this was a clear and recognized feature of marriage as seen by Catholics.

Those who contract marriage for morally indifferent reasons extrinsic to marriage are usually excused from venial sin, because they usually choose them, not as their aims in marriage but as the reason for bethinking them-

[7] *In 4 Sent.*, d. 31, q. 1, a. 3.

selves of marriage, or of marriage to one particular person. The aim of their marriage is still the proper one even if they do not give it any thought. Unless they expressly exclude the proper aim, they intend it virtually and implicitly by the very fact that they intend to contract marriage. . . .

Nor in the marriage act itself is there any need to recall some one of the permissible aims. It is enough if the act is habitually related to them, just as, according to the common opinion of theologians, this is sufficient for merit. . . . Thus it is enough if in the beginning the couple enter upon marriage with them in mind and have no contrary aim in the act itself. . . . This is why Ledesma says that married people are excused from many venial sins. . . .

From this we deduce that a husband making use of marriage and neither expressly intending nor excluding children but simply unmindful of them and intent solely on having relations with his wife because she is his wife, in no way sins. Granted that he does not intend children formally, he does intend them virtually, since that act, by its own very nature, is designed for the procreation of children, and the performer's intention is not directing it to any other aim.[8]

Notice how carefully these more lenient principles were integrated with the old supposition that venereal pleasure is inherently evil. This was the basic assumption of all studies of marriage once Augustine expressed it so cogently.

And yet at the same time and in the same studies, conclusions began to appear which were actually at variance with that assumption. During the 1100's more than one theologian was careful to point out that pleasure is not necessarily sinful. It proceeds from a

[8] *De Sac. Mat.*, lib. 2, disp. 29, nn. 24-5; lib. 9, disp. 8, nn. 3-4.

nature which is still essentially good despite the damage done by original sin. Some noted that this is just as true of sexual pleasure.

William of Auxerre, who edited Aristotle for students of the early 1200's, explains that sexual pleasure would exist even if Adam had never fallen. Albert the Great goes on to say that intercourse is now a reminder of sin, not because it involves a certain pleasure, but because that pleasure is not as great as it would have been.

I readily concede that there would have been a greater and more sincere pleasure in the act then; and yet it would have been under the control of reason. For reason was then strengthened by the grace of innocence. Nothing inferior to it, no matter how intense it might have been, would have turned it from contemplating the changeless First Good.[9]

Thus if there is any sin in sexual relations, it is due, not to the pleasure but to some disorder in the way pleasure is experienced.

Demetrius Cydones, secretary to the Patriarch of Constantinople, was converted from schism, studied Aquinas extensively and translated his works into Greek. As though this were not unusual enough, his views on sexual pleasure have been found in a work called *Despising Death*. Remarking that some might rebel at the thought of no longer knowing the joys of marriage, he reminded them of why these things exist.

He devised them for parents so that men would be more prompt to see that there were children to take their place.

[9] *In 4 Sent.*, d. 26, a. 7.

Pleasure tends to make them forget the inconveniences, which result from having a family. We see . . . doctors, even harsh ones, . . . mix certain sweetenings with their bitterest preparations so that people, intent on the sweet, will more easily take the medicines as well.[10]

Though regarded as perfectly orthodox after his conversion, and imbued by his studies of Aquinas with the spirit of Latin theology, this writer was not so strongly affected by it because of his background. And not long after his death in 1400, it became apparent that he was not as different as might have been expected from Latin theologians of the time. In Flanders, Denis the Carthusian explains that

Since a husband and wife can have relations without sin and virtuously, as has been said, there is a legitimate carnal love. They love each other because of the pleasure they have in and from each other to the extent that pleasure is natural, joined to the marriage act by God's providence, and related to a proper aim.
As Aristotle says and St. Thomas repeats, our moral evaluation of an act and of the pleasure joined to an act is the same. Therefore the pleasure from a good and virtuous act is good; and to the extent that it is good, it can be desired.[11]

By the following century it was apparent that this view had blended with that of Cydones. According to Charles V's theologian at Trent, Dominic Soto,

Nature has wisely attached pleasure to that act because of the need to conserve the race. . . . Therefore just as taking

[10] De Cond. Morte, c. 6, PG 154, 1179-1182.
[11] De Laudabili Vita Conjugatorum, a. 8.

one's food and drink with pleasure is no sin, neither is
marital intercourse.

And certainly those who say the contrary, in other words,
that it is a sin unless a man abhors the pleasure involved,
are trying to deprive men of their natural feeling. The mind
is simply not able to elicit displeasure in that situation.[12]

Alfonso Salmeron, one of the pope's own theologians
at Trent, not only shared this view but tried to settle
a difficulty which had bothered so many. If this
pleasure is good, why is there an instinctive embarrassment about sexual relations?

He answers with earlier writers that it indicates, not
a sin but a punishment, and then observes, "Christ the
Lord has not taken away the embarrassment about
this matter so that the embarrassment itself would be
a restraint on intercourse."[13]

It is not a proof that the sex instinct is evil. It is a
protection against an evil more basic than the sex
instinct: the lawlessness of fallen human nature.

From this time on it was clear even from those who
wrote in the spirit of Augustine that Catholics no
longer saw the matter as he had. Jean Grou, a spiritual
director whose spirit and ideas were those of Augustine, moved on to conclusions which reflected the more
nuanced view of later generations.

As for the marriage act, man would naturally have some
aversion for it and would never be borne by pure reason
to take up a state so enslaving, so hard to bear as marriage
were it not accompanied by some pleasure attractive to the

[12] *In 4 Sent.*, d. 31, q. 1, n. 3.
[13] *Commentarii in Evangelicam Historiam*, 5, tr. 9, p. 50.

that state, it offered those that the schoolmen had agreed upon but then reflected the view of later writers like Soto or Salmeron.

If to these reasons are also added others which induce men to enter marriage and, in making the choice of a wife, to prefer this one to that—the desire of leaving an heir, wealth, beauty, the prominence of the family, similar tastes and habits—these reasons are certainly not to be condemned, since they are not opposed to the holiness of marriage. In sacred scripture the Patriarch Jacob is not reprehended for being allured by Rachel's beauty and preferring her to Lia.[19]

What this would imply about intercourse itself was stated clearly some years later by Sanchez. Love for the other is a perfectly licit motive, not only for marrying in the first place but for having marital relations.
St. Francis de Sales explained this directly to laymen.

To eat with no thought of preserving life but simply with a view to maintaining the companionship and affability we owe one another is something very just and honorable. By the same token, the reciprocal and legitimate satisfaction of the partners to a holy marriage is called by St. Paul a debt, and a debt so great that he does not want one of the partners to exempt himself from it without the free and ready consent of the other, not even for the exercises of devotion. . . .[20]

This attention to sexual intercourse as an expression of a married couple's whole attitude toward each other

[19] Cat. Conc. Trid., II, 8, 14.
[20] Introd. Vie Dev., p. 3, c. 39.

and a help to keeping it unchanged was evident toward the end of the eighteenth century in the works of Jean Grou, whose popularity as a spiritual director was not due to any laxity in his opinions. During the nineteenth century, seminarians, who would eventually be directing married couples, were taught by more than one textbook.

If they have relations to foster their love for each other, to ease any suspicions that love is growing cold, or for other such reasons, these aims are not alien to the use of marriage. They are reducible to fidelity, which is a distinctive asset of that state.[21]

Moralists of the present century agree. "Intercourse may honorably be sought . . . to show one's love."[22] An authoritative statement of how the matter appears to Catholics is furnished by Pius XI's encyclical on marriage.

Both in marriage itself and in the use of marital rights there are also secondary aims such as . . . fostering mutual love . . . which married people are in no way forbidden to seek, as long as the intrinsic nature of the act, and hence its right order to the primary aim, is always secure.[23]

Thus the very fact which gave rise to all the difficulty, a distinctive pleasure of the senses, emerges as almost incidental to the intercourse of husband and wife. For them the experience is more than a biological mating.

[21] Dominic Palmieri, S.J., *Tractatus de Matrimonio Christiano*, Rome: S.C. de Propag. Fide, 1880, tr. 10, c. 2, p. 289.
[22] Arthur Vermeersch, S.J., *De Castitate*, Rome: P.U.G., 1921, ed. 2a, p. 224.
[23] *Casti Connubbi*, AAS 22 (1930), 561.

It is the response of a person to a person. There is tremendous satisfaction, but its source is something noble, distinctively human, and emphatically Christian: a sincere and unselfish love.

What the Church has known about human sexuality will thus be apparent from the way it has reacted to a historical situation, or rather to two historical facts: the culture of the lands in which most Catholics have lived, and the awareness felt by each adult Catholic of a tendency deep within to have no regard for God, other persons, anything but himself.

Confronted with that twofold situation and appraising it in the light of Christ, how has the Church reacted? As for explicit statements about the sex instinct, it is obvious that there has been a tremendous change. Only a sleight of hand with the documents can make Augustine, Aquinas and Pius XII say the same things. Once the Church had moved out of Palestine, all study and speculation took place in an ancient pagan culture which had an ingrained suspicion of matter and pleasure. Augustine not only grew up in this atmosphere but for several years was even a Manichaean. And his was the theology handed down to Western Europe. The Schoolmen received it hallowed by time, enhanced by the absence of any comparable body of thought since his death, and strengthened by a few spurious documents which gave it more official sanction than it really had. Blending with the Graeco-Roman concept of man which they were discovering in the pages of Aristotle, it could not help but affect their view of what Christ had revealed.

During all this time, however, there were forces pulling from the opposite direction. Cultures change with glacial slowness, but the more the Christian view of life actually dominated the age in which they lived, the more Christian writers seem to have changed. And the more they modified what they read by what they saw, the more pronounced the change appears.

The Church's intellectual life depends, as we have noticed, on a continual dialogue. The faithful receive a general set of values which they apply to practical daily living, and the theologians keep refining general theories to fit the actual life which they see, not among those who persist in doing what they continually hear is wrong, such as couples today who use contraceptives, but among the great mass of "good Catholics" who assume that they are doing all they should.

When we speak of tradition we must consider both participants in this dialogue; and if we do, it becomes apparent that the Catholic tradition on human sexuality has been an ever growing appreciation of insights possessed from the beginning.

The same prudential knowledge from which the faithful were acting told the theologians that the faithful were right. Since they were obviously not on a pagan quest of pleasure and yet were not always thinking of children either, there must be other reasons which justified their conduct. These other reasons gradually found their way into the books—keeping the other from sin, rendering the debt, allaying concupiscence, fostering mutual love. As formulas were gradually modified to express what is right, the descriptions of marriage gradually changed to show why it is right.

Few things are more basic to a culture than its concept

of the relationship between man and woman. Since the deepest emotions and the most intimate details of life are involved, the thought of many generations has usually been expended on the subject, and few convictions are more impatient of any disturbance. The change in what Christian writers said from the second till the twentieth century reflects nothing so much as a struggle between two cultural views on human sexuality with the Christian view gradually prevailing.

This Christian view discloses certain truths about human life as Christ reveals it. First, the tendency that each of us feels to make himself the axis around which the rest of the world revolves, to use other men and even God to his own advantage, is the result of a primal sin which has made us inheritors of a damaged human nature. But though sexual intercourse is one occasion when that unruly tendency displays itself, the sex instinct is not the result of original sin. Much less is it the continuation of rebellion. Both the instinct and its expression in marriage are features of human life as God designed it.

Nor is there any warrant for thinking that this part of human nature has been more severely damaged than the rest. The orientation of man and woman toward each other is not simply "man's lower nature." If revelation shows that this orientation has been affected by original sin, the reaction it suggests is not shame, but modesty, an impulse to protect what is good, a fear of desecrating something holy, a reserve about a part of life as personal as prayer.

Granted that husband and wife as a rule have their

whole attention on each other, this does not mean that God's design is thwarted. The process has a built-in purpose, but it does not follow that they must have this purpose in mind. Since the term of the process is not an animal but a human being, God may conceivably intend that this term result from a certain psychological state of two other human beings.

As a matter of fact, this is the distinctive feature of human sexuality. The rigorist errs as badly as the libertine when he describes the intercourse of husband and wife in terms of physical pleasure. That particular activity of a human being is supposed to say something. It is essentially a gesture. Just as words are designed to convey thought, this gesture has been devised by the the Creator as the expression of a unique attitude toward another human being. As real and essential as the connection with life is its connection with love.

Thus, in addition to being the source of human life, a fact which calls for certain restraints, sexual intercourse has another function, no less intrinsic, no less designed by God; and this too demands certain restraints. The expression of love must never become an expression of selfishness.

But the good man is not the one who is insensitive to sexual stimuli. He is the one who makes a reasonable effort to avoid them outside of the proper time. If his instincts happen to be weak, this is no more an asset than if he had no taste for food, no appreciation of music. Neither marriage itself nor the instinct which prompts it needs any apology. They are from God.

Marriage and Sexuality: The Catholic Position

JOHN L. THOMAS, S.J.

Human love, "the way of a man with a maid," will always remain something of a mystery—we will never quite understand what Jack sees in Jill or *vice versa*. Yet love also includes some self-evident qualities it would be fatal to ignore. Conjugal love, human love *par excellence,* is inherently related to human sexuality, and experience suggests that human sexual desires and impulses are not automatically regulated either by the demands of love or the parental abilities of the couple. Because of its profound personal and social consequences, we must face the fact that like all other living species the human race is endowed with an amazing procreative capacity. If this reproductive potential is fully actualized in marriage, or if death resulting from disease, famine and war does not eliminate a considerable percentage of offspring particularly before they can reproduce, human populations will grow rapidly, while individual couples will find it increasingly difficult to reconcile the normal expressions of their love with the requirements of the moral law.

SOCIAL CHANGE

Now it is something of an open secret that many contemporary Catholic couples are experiencing serious difficulties in this regard. Remarkable advances in health care, accompanied by rapid changes in our social system and marriage patterns, have profoundly modified traditional responsibilities and attitudes relating to the bearing and rearing of children. Although the long history of contraception, sterilization, abortion, and infanticide clearly indicates that there have always been some individuals or groups who for various reasons have attempted to frustrate or eliminate the normal outcome of sexual relations, throughout much of the past it was generally assumed that the average couple were able to bear and rear all the children they might be privileged to have throughout the course of their marriage. Under contemporary conditions, given the current relatively early age at marriage, widespread emphasis on sexual stimulation and expression, high standards of health care, increasing costs, and added length of formal training required to prepare youth for adequate participation in our technically advanced society, many fertile young couples must face realistically the serious challenge of spacing pregnancies and regulating the size of their families.

Meanwhile, the developments in the medical and

biological sciences that have made possible our remarkable advances in health care have also greatly
increased our understanding of the human reproductive process. Of special interest to Catholic couples in
particular, the discovery of fairly reliable means of
predicting or ascertaining the fertile and sterile periods
of the normal menstrual cycle offers the possibility of
exercising considerable control over conception. Although much remains to be discovered concerning
various aspects of this highly complex process, intelligent use of currently available knowledge would enable most couples to influence their reproductive
patterns substantially. Thus, by directing the use of
their marital rights in accordance with the observed
rhythm of the wife's fertile and sterile periods, couples
are able to increase or minimize their chances of
conceiving.

A further significant aspect of the contemporary situation is that in our morally pluralist, highly secular
society members of the Christian minority must solve
their family problems within a framework of beliefs,
values and norms no longer recognized as valid by
most of their contemporaries. For all practical purposes this means that Catholic couples must work out
their salvation within a social system geared to the
small family and patterned on the assumption that
contraceptive birth control will be widely used. The
continued observance of Christian marriage norms
under such circumstances appears at all likely only if
Catholic couples acquire an adequate understanding
and appreciation of the Church's positive doctrine

concerning the vocation of marriage, together with
the firm conviction that this doctrine is currently
relevant.

Marriage generates and fulfills a number of not easily
postponable wants. If Catholic couples cannot discover effective and morally acceptable solutions to
problems seriously affecting their marital happiness,
experience suggests that they will tend to adopt secular
solutions, meanwhile justifying such decisions on the
premise that God does not expect the impossible.
Granting the relative newness, complexity and magni-
tude of the present challenge, therefore, it seems
obvious that only a consistently integrated program
which takes into consideration both the natural and
supernatural dimensions of the problem, courageously
subjects traditional conceptions and attitudes to a profound reappraisal, and bases its practical proposals on
a realistic understanding of the varied pressures and
pulls currently experienced by Catholic couples, will
prove really effective.

THE NATURE OF HUMAN SEXUALITY

An adequately comprehensive view of human sexuality must keep in careful focus the physical facts, their
individual and social implications, and their significance or meaning as culturally defined. Human
sexuality is such a complex phenomenon not only
because it implies disjunctive though complementary
personal attributes (bisexuality) and consequently
couple-centered fulfillment, but also because the basic

function with which it is associated (the procreation and education of offspring) is closely related to group continuity and survival. Since there is substantial evidence that many past and current interpretations of sex reflect partial, segmented, or unintegrated conceptual frames of reference, it may prove useful to recall briefly a few facts about human sexuality before proceeding further.

In the first place, sex, defined as the possession of a reproductively incomplete though mutually complementary generative system, has profound implications for men and women. Considered from the viewpoint of the person, sex involves both individual and social aspects, that is, it is a way of being-to-the-world and of being-to-others. Its individual aspect is reflected at all levels of the person's activity: psycho-physical (genital), psycho-social (masculinity and femininity), and spiritual (transcendental and supernatural). Its social aspect is reflected in the sexually specific, culturally defined statuses and roles in terms of which boys and girls are trained and which later determine their relative positions, accepted areas of activity, and aspirational goals in the adult community. Considered from the viewpoint of society or the group, sex appears as the basis of that primary human community of life and love designed to provide for the orderly fulfillment of man's sexually associated needs and to guarantee the adequate recruitment of new members.

Second, recent research on the functioning of the major motivational systems in man indicates that the central neural mechanisms controlling the sexual drive are not dependent on physiological maturation or seasonal physiological changes in his endocrine glands; and that even when sexually aroused, his sexual goal-behavior is not innate or "built-in" but is the product of learning. This helps explain the variety of reported sexual practices in the human species, as well as the occurrence of so-called sexual perversions. The fact that man does not possess a "sexual instinct," in the sense that he inherits no innate desire to accomplish any specific behavioral goal in this regard, underlines the significance of cultural definition and learning, while the fact that his brain mechanisms controlling sexual arousal are independent of control by the late maturing endocrine glands considerably enlarges the scope of his freedom and responsibility in sex relations.

Third, the existence of fully functioning sexual-arousal mechanisms in all normal human beings from childhood to old age, together with the fact that the personality development of individuals progresses through definite stages, must inevitably give rise to numerous challenges relating to sex education and the internalizing of appropriate controls. It also renders necessary the determination, establishment, and socially sanctioned regulation of appropriate premarital, marital and extramarital cross-sex relationships. Basically, of course, it requires the formulation of an integrated philosophy of sex that takes full account not only of its physiological and psychological mechanisms but also of the personal, social and moral implications necessarily involved in its use as an unique expression of human love and procreativity.

Finally, human sexual response and receptivity are not

dependent on seasonal or cyclical physiological changes relating to the couple's glandular systems or to ovulation. In sharp contrast to all but perhaps a few of the higher mammals, human partners are always sexually accessible to each other; that is, they can be sexually responsive and receptive at all times. Specifically, although the reproductively mature human female is capable of conceiving during only a relatively brief period (15 to 20 hours) in each menstrual cycle, the human couple have been granted no direct knowledge of the precise time of ovulation and remain sexually responsive and receptive throughout the entire cycle. Thus if we consider this aspect of human sexuality from the perspective of natural law, we must conclude that in making the human couple as He did, the Creator clearly intended that marital relations were to serve to a significant degree both *relational* and *procreational* functions.

In other words, proceeding on the basic assumption of natural law theory that we can discover the divine law by studying the natures of things as revealed in their normal operations, our study of man's reproductive systems (masculine and feminine) and their normal operations shows that the human couple must normally engage in a series of marital acts if they wish to procreate. Contrary to most past opinion, the failure of the non-pregnant wife to conceive in every act of intercourse is owing not to some "defect of nature" but indicates divine intent as revealed in the normal functioning of her generative system. Hence we conclude that in creating the human female with an ovulation cycle that renders her capable of conception during only a relatively brief period in each menstrual cycle, while at the same time endowing the human couple with no direct means of knowing when ovulation occurs, the Creator obviously intended sexual relations to serve a significant unifying (relational) function in marriage. Stated negatively, in providing for the propagation of the human race, the Creator did not create the human couple with the same type of reproductive systems as the other animals; in particular, the human female does not experience the typical mammalian seasonal or cyclical oestrus during which period alone she is sexually receptive, nor does the act of human intercourse induce ovulation as sexual congress apparently does among some animals.

On the basis of these observations, we conclude that it would appear more in keeping with the presently known facts to maintain that not the individual act of intercourse but what might be called the *process of sexual relations* is procreative. This would seem to call for some reappraisal of traditional views relating to the significance of the relational and procreational functions of marital relations. Although other influences were probably operative, an analysis of the inadequate knowledge of the human reproductive system available to the great theologians who formulated the basic principles guiding later Christian thought in this regard suggests that this was the major factor accounting for their amazing disregard of the relational function. The result has been a quasi-fixation on the procreational function, an unrealistic readiness to recommend absolute continency or relatively long periods of sexual abstinence in marriage, the justification of marital relations during sterile periods more or less as a concession to fallen nature (*remedium concupiscentiae* negatively defined), and in general, a remarkable devaluation of marital sexual activity for purposes other than procreation or the apparently unilateral (male) allaying of desire.

SEXUALITY AND MARRIAGE

Because uninhibited or unintegrated expressions of sex result in conduct disruptive of individual and social well-being, all known societies have had to face the challenge of formulating workable systems of control. Essentially, the problem consists in reconciling the need for control with the need for expression. Social order demands control; group continuity and personal fulfillment require expression. Considering the complexity of the personal and social factors involved, as well as the various ways in which men can regard human nature and its sexual functions, it is not surprising to find that societies differ considerably in the prohibitions and permissions they develop. Historically, there have been two major systems of control, distinguished by their focus of interest—society-centered or person-centered. The former is common to most cultures outside the Judaic and Christian spheres of influence; the latter has been characteristic of our Western approach.

The fundamental premise underlying the Catholic view of sexual morality is that there exists an essential relationship between the use of sex and marriage. To the extent that human sexual activity is the conscious, voluntary act of a responsible individual, it can achieve its full value and significance only if it is conjugal, that is, only if it is the expression and actualization of that community of life and love established by the human couple in marriage. The basic principle involved here can be stated briefly: ". . . by the law of God and of nature, every use of the faculty given by God for the procreation of new life is the right and the privilege of the marriage state alone and must be confined absolutely with the sacred limits of that state."[1] In other words, if by their very nature the generative faculties are essentially related to the process of reproduction, with all this activity implies in terms of the care and education of children, then the right and privilege of using these faculties must be confined to couples who by their mutual agreement have bound themselves to establish the type of enduring society in which children can be fittingly reared to maturity.

Applying this principle with remarkable consistency down through the centuries, Catholic theologians have formulated a relatively complete set of moral controls relating to the use of sex. In general, two basic concerns have dominated their thinking: first, the protection of human life in any and every form—hence their strong condemnation of abortion and infanticide; second, respect for nature, that is, the recognition and

[1] Pius XI, Encyclical, *On Christian Marriage*.

acceptance of the need to maintain the integrity of the inherent structure of the sexual act—hence their condemnation of all and sundry contraceptive techniques.

According to their positive teaching, chastity is the virtue that regulates the use of sex in conformity with right reason, and as such it may be regarded as a form of the cardinal virtue of temperance, the general virtue pertaining to the human appetites having to do with the pleasures of eating, drinking, sense of touch, and so forth. Thus the chaste person is one who realizes the order of reason (the order that corresponds to the reality made evident to man through both human knowledge and faith) in the use of sex, while sins against chastity are transgressions or violations of right order in this regard. Briefly, taking into consideration the origin, nature, and destiny of man, together with the nature and purpose of his reproductive system, they conclude that right order requires that all voluntary expressions of the sensitive appetite for venereal pleasure must be avoided by the unmarried and be regulated in conformity with the ends of marriage and the purposes of the generative act in the marital state.

THE OBJECTIVE ENDS OF MARRIAGE

We learn from the opening chapters of Genesis that the Creator designed the dual sexual nature of man with a double finality—parenthood and mutual fulfillment through a loving life-partnership. Since marriage

is a natural institution based on the bisexual nature of
man, we conclude that the Creator ordained it to
achieve this double finality and consequently intends
it to be a community of life and love through which
the human couple are to seek their mutual fulfillment
and perfection in His service by dedicating themselves
to a special mission, the procreation and education of
children. Christian thinkers have employed various
expressions in stating this double finality of marriage.
Thus St. Augustine formulated his classic definition
of the "goods" of marriage in the famous trilogy:
conjugal fidelity, children, and indissoluble union.
Centuries later, when explaining "the reasons because
of which man and woman ought to be joined in marriage," the catechism of the Council of Trent declares:
"The first is precisely the companionship sought by
the natural instinct of different sex, and brought about
in the hope of mutual aid, so that each may help the
other to bear more easily the troubles of life, and to
support the weakness of old age. The second is the
desire of having children."

The present Code of Canon Law, employing a somewhat more precise legal approach, states that the
primary purpose of marriage is the procreation and
education of children, while its twofold secondary
purpose is mutual service and the remedy of concupiscence.[2] Although the Code follows long-standing
theological and canon law usage when employing the
expression *primary purpose* here, this technical term
has all too frequently been interpreted out of context,

[2] Canon 1013, No. 1.

particularly in what we might call the "taught" tradition, that is, the content of beliefs actually communicated to the faithful through sermons, schools, popular writing and folklore. The major resultant misunderstandings stem primarily from misinterpretations relating to the following points.

First, the primary purpose of marriage (procreation and education of offspring) constitutes one purpose—not two. In the moral order the procreation of a child is inseparable from the obligation to educate it, because God confides the human infant to its parents not as an adult but as a person-to-be-developed. By its very nature the marriage contract binds the couple to work together for the establishment of a stable, loving society or "home" in which children can be fittingly conceived, born, and reared to Christian maturity. Procreation constitutes but the first stage in this total process of fulfilling the primary purpose of marriage.

Second, when we state that this integral procreation-education process constitutes the *primary* purpose of marriage, we mean that it is the specifying purpose or end distinguishing marriage from all other possible types of association or partnership between man and woman (brother-sister, father-daughter, housekeeper-boarder, and so on). These other types of partnership may supply many of the services normally provided by marriage, yet they are clearly distinguished from marriage because they do not involve the valid exchange of marital rights. Only marriage places the couple in a procreative status, that is, in a state of life conferring both the mutual, exclusive, and perpetual right to acts that are in their very nature apt for begetting children, and the corresponding obligation relating to the responsible exercise of this right.

Third, both the primary and secondary purposes of marriage are *objective* purposes, that is, they are ends inherent in the very structure of marriage. The terms *primary* and *secondary* are here used in a strictly technical sense, that is, to indicate the order or rank existing among the several objective ends and how they are interrelated. Thus "mutual service" and "the remedy of concupiscence" are *secondary* purposes in the sense that they are designed to make the primary purpose (the procreation-education process) more easily and adequately achieved.

Fourth, marital relations also are secondary or subordinate to the primary purpose of marriage (the integral procreation-education process). This means that if the couple choose to engage in marital relations, they must respect both the integrity of the inherent structure of the act (use no contraceptive obstacle to interfere with the physiological process they have voluntarily initiated), and its subordination to the primary purpose of marriage; that is, the act must be used not selfishly, but to strengthen their union and thus enable them to fulfill their roles as partners and parents more perfectly. This subordination of marital relations to the primary purpose of marriage has often been very inadequately defined, if not seriously misconceived. Owing not only to the failure to understand the divinely intended unifying relational function of marital relations but also to the tendency to define the primary purpose of marriage simply as "procreation," major emphasis in discussing the use of marital rights usually focuses either on the evils of contraception, the obligations relating to the *debitum*, or the psychologically tardy assurance that "sex" is good in marriage and should be enjoyed.

Finally, the primary purpose of marriage does not imply either as an ideal or as a safe moral norm that couples should have as many children as they are biologically capable of producing. As a humanly responsible act, procreation necessarily implies the sincere assumption of the grave obligations involved in the total process of bearing and rearing children. Although all couples must bring the complete dedication of themselves to their marriage, each couple will differ in their capacity to fulfill its primary purpose. For various reasons, some may have no children, or not as many as they may desire, while others will have to judge prudently how many they can reasonably bear and raise to Christian maturity. This decision must be made within the moral framework of their purpose in life and the obligations of the special vocation, but the responsibility of making it must rest with the individual couple concerned.

In the practical order this means that couples entering marriage have the right and obligation to be adequately informed concerning the moral conditions required for making a prudent judgment in this regard, and they should have ready access to reliable information concerning the licit means of regulating family size currently available. Unfortunately, although the Church's teaching relating to the morality of family regulation is clear enough, misunderstanding and confusion remain prevalent in the "taught" tradition, while both the medical and lay sources of information concerning workable means are frustratingly inadequate if not inept.

Family Size, Rhythm, and the Pill

RICHARD A. McCORMICK, S.J.

The common denominator of the three entries mentioned in the above title is: family regulation and limitation. The notions of family regulation and family limitation are not new; but their emergence as problems involving intense Catholic concern at all levels is relatively new. The reasons for this are largely twofold.

First of all, it is only in the past thirty years that regulation of birth through the practice of rhythm has become a practical possibility. Before this time the cyclic character of reproductive capacity was known, but unfortunately until the independent discoveries of Ogino and Knaus the mid-cycle period was widely regarded as the sterile period. The many disappointments consequent upon this confusion meant that the only reliable methods of family regulation were contraception and total abstinence. Because both alternatives represented a way of life with which the ordinary Catholic would experience grave difficulties, the problems of family limitation and regulation remained somewhat academic at least as a matter of common concern.

Secondly, the clarification of reproductive physiology making rhythm possible for many has been accompanied by modern cultural and economic developments making its use often desirable, even necessary.[1] The tendency of modern couples to marry young and begin their families immediately means an increased span of fertility. Infant and child mortality has decreased dramatically in the past half decade, partially at least through costly medical care and hospitalization. Enormous technological advancement has brought higher and more expensive levels of material living and simultaneously longer, more demanding, and more expensive educational requirements. American society experiences increasingly the employment of the mother outside the home, the mobility of younger couples (fostering economic independence from family and relatives), the uncertainties associated with service in the armed forces. Furthermore, there is an ever more acute awareness of and interest in the population problems of underdeveloped countries. Modern contraceptive values and programs have achieved a widespread publicity and acceptance. This concentration of events has made family planning a major practical issue for individual couples and an area of intense awareness on the part of the Catholic community.

It is not surprising that there is deep Catholic concern

[1] Cf. John L. Thomas, S.J., *The Catholic Viewpoint on Marriage and the Family* (New York: Hanover, 1958), pp. 144-145.

over problems of family planning. These problems affect not only the material well-being of nations and communities; they relate closely to conjugal intimacy, to growth in conjugal love, to the achievement of cojugal chastity—in a word, to the health, happiness, and stability of marriage itself. The Catholic seeks and deserves to find in his values and traditions guidance which will help him solve his problems of sexual expression within the structure of the highest Christian principles.

FAMILY SIZE

In the popular mind the Catholic Church is associated with the ideal of the large family. There are possibly many reasons for this. First of all, the Church's statements that procreation and education of children are the primary end of marriage and her open disapproval of attempts to attribute primacy to personalist values have often been uncritically interpreted. Her rejection of direct abortion has led many to conclude erroneously that she prefers the child to the mother. Further, the many papal allusions to children and large families as a blessing are well known. The Church not only rejects contraception and direct sterilization but teaches a positive obligation to procreate. Traditionally, the "procreative criterion" has functioned pivotally in her explanation and defense of sexual morality. In early scholastic theology, from which traditional explanations of sexual morality borrow heavily, the concept of procreation is almost uniquely and sometimes erroneously the sole criterion of morality. Many of our large families are in fact Catholic. Finally, popular association of the phrase "responsible parenthood" with the theology of those who sanction contraception has tended to identify many Catholics as irresponsible members of the procreative set.

To characterize the large family as the Catholic ideal of family size is a dangerous oversimplification, probably the result of many assumptions and oversights. It fails to assess the implications of the fact that procreation *and education* are presented as the primary end of marriage. Furthermore, it makes unjustified assumptions about the meaning of the difficult terms primary and secondary, and forgets the interdependence of these two ends. It neglects the fact that the Church, while she teaches a positive duty to procreate, insists that there are excusing causes "in truth very wide" from such a duty and hopes that the rhythm method may find an even more secure medical basis. It overlooks repeated papal insistence that the conjugal act can only be viewed and judged adequately in its totality. It fails to weigh carefully the implications of the rejection of homologous artificial insemination and the essential and heavy emphasis placed on personal values in marriage and conjugal intimacy by authentic Catholic teaching. It forgets that although papal literature speaks of children as a blessing and warms appreciatively to the image of the large family, this literature supposes the existence of individual circumstances which will make these an advantage both to married partners and the child.

It is not too strong to refer to "papal insistence that the conjugal act can only be viewed and judged adequately in its totality." After condemning artificial insemination even within marriage (that is, any procedure which is a substitute for natural intercourse) in an address to the fourth International Convention of Catholic Doctors,[2] Pius XII returned to the subject in his Address to the Midwives:

To reduce the cohabitation of married persons and the conjugal act to a mere organic function for the transmission of the germ of life would be to convert the domestic hearth, sanctuary of the family, into nothing more than a biological laboratory. Hence, in our address of September 29, 1949, to the international congress of Catholic doctors, we formally excluded artificial insemination from marriage. The conjugal act in its natural structure is a personal action, a simultaneous and immediate cooperation of the spouses which, by the very nature of the agents and the character of the act, expresses that mutual self-donation which, in the words of Holy Scripture, effects the union "in one flesh."

This is much more than the mere union of two life-germs, which can be brought about also artificially, that is, without the natural action of the spouses. The conjugal act, as it is planned and willed by nature, is a personal cooperation, the right to which the parties have mutually conferred on each other in contracting marriage.[3]

[2] *AAS 41* (1949), 559-561.
[3] *AAS 43* (1951), 850.

Later, in 1956, in his address to the Second World Congress on Fertility and Sterility, Pius XII wrote:

But the Church has likewise rejected the opposite attitude which would pretend to separate, in generation, the biological activity from the personal relation of the married couple. The child is the fruit of the conjugal union when that union finds full expression by bringing into play the organic functions, the associated sensible emotions, and the spiritual and disinterested love which animates it. It is within the unity of this human activity that the biological prerequisites of generation should take place. Never is it permitted to separate these various aspects to the point of excluding positively either the procreative scope or the conjugal embrace. The relationship which unites the father and the mother to their child finds its true fulfillment in the being which they bring into the world. Furthermore, only this consecration of self, generous in its origin, arduous in its realization, can guarantee, through the conscious acceptance of the responsibilities which it involves, that the task of educating the children will be pursued with all the care and courage and patience which it demands.[4]

Actually, if there exists a Catholic position on family size, it must be simply an explicitation of the Catholic view on marriage and conjugal love. Such a position avoids the extremes implicit in absolutist over-simplifications. While Catholic teaching rejects the secularist pursuit of personal comforts to the neglect of offspring as an inversion of values and an attack on conjugal life and love, it attributes on the other hand no absolute value to mere quantity. Quantity (small or large) neither implies nor precludes quality. If

[4] *AAS 48* (1956), 470.

children within a family are praised as a blessing, this is so only in so far as it is supposed in the concrete case that they would make growth in conjugal love (hence also their own education) more likely. The Church has too much respect for the sanctity of marriage, the happiness and sanctification of the individual couple, the individual conscience, the operations of the Holy Spirit, and the well-being of the children to propose an absolute, quantitative norm of largeness or smallness as something to which all or most couples should aspire. This absolutist mentality would compromise the very values she regards as essential to both marriage and conjugal love.

Rather than propose a quantitative ideal, the Catholic Church explains all aspects and values of Christian married life and love and proposes these as the essential structure within which the individual couple should make its own decisions. The Church does not and cannot make the decision for the couple. But from an enormous experience she realizes that the characteristic threat to such a decision is an inversion of values and her emphasis often reflects this awareness. She realizes that this decision, as relative to individual circumstances and therefore highly dynamic (subject to constant revaluation), should be made in creative awareness to her own general proposals, the circumstance of the individual situation, and the inspirations of the Holy Spirit—and therefore in Christian prudence in the fullest sense. Some couples will prayerfully conclude that it is best for them to have large families in so far as this is in their control; others will conclude to the need of some regulation, even limitation over long periods; still others may regretfully decide that it is impossible for them to raise a family. As long as the decision is the product of *Christian* prudence, the Church regards this as responsible parenthood. And it is precisely responsible parenthood which best characterizes her attitude about family size since only responsible parenthood will secure the values regarded as essential by Catholic teaching.

RHYTHM

The individual circumstances of many couples will lead them to conclude to the need of spacing or limiting their children, or perhaps even of completely excluding offspring. Yet they understandably desire and feel the need to continue regular marital intimacy. Since Catholic teaching regards the conjugal act "as given" as an act of procreative love and demands fidelity to this given pattern in the individual act, the only morally acceptable way (thus far known) of implementing the decision to regulate the number of children is through periodic continence, or rhythm. Rhythm is the systematic practice of restricting intercourse to the sterile periods for the purpose of avoiding conception.

The practice of rhythm is essentially different from contraceptive procedures. This difference has regrettably all too often failed to reach the popular level where identity of physical effects (avoidance of pregnancy) is accepted as identity of moral acts, a confusion which can lead to the conviction that rhythm is equivalently contraception, or eventually to the acceptance of contraception itself. The difficulty of many conscientious Catholics in understanding traditional insistence on the procreative character of individual acts (sc., that nothing is done to prevent the meeting of ovum and sperm) is itself one of the major pastoral problems in the practice of periodic continence. The partial independence of the two areas (biological conception, personal sexual union) causes many doubts. In most cases of marital union conception is not possible; yet the inclination to union is present indicating that possibility of conception and inclination to union are not parallel. Does this not indicate that the specifying character of the act is primarily mutual love? Furthermore, how can the marriage act be called procreative when procreation takes place later than the marriage act? How is it procreative when one or both partners are sterile? Or when the sterile periods are deliberately chosen to avoid conception?

Yet Catholic teaching insists that the marital act is essentially (and therefore must remain) an act of procreative love. To grasp the traditional Catholic position on rhythm and its difference from contraception, one must understand what is meant by the "procreative character" of the marital act. To understand this *adequately* (sc. in a manner which avoids a unilateral, apparently biologistic emphasis) one must further understand the over-all Catholic attitude toward the act of sexual intercourse.

Theologians view the sexual act as an act of procreative love, as a personal, loving communion with a specific procreative character. That is, the marital embrace "as given" or according to its given pattern has two essential characteristics: it is (1) an expression of love and (2) procreative. These characteristics theologians call *fines operis*, or perhaps, essential inner senses of the act.

The act of conjugal love is procreative. This is a conclusion from the over-all reproductive orientation of sexuality in general. This orientation is a matter of basic observation, the type of thing which is probably impervious to rational proof, yet so clear that the attempt at proof comes off a bit ridiculous. As the eminent priest-psychiatrist Marc Oraison notes:

It cannot be too often emphasized that sexuality in the living world has for its specific role the reproduction of the species. And anyone who does not, in his reflections on this subject, set out from this elementary fact or does not take it into strict account would run the serious risk of losing touch with the most fundamental data on the matter.[5]

As an actuation of a productive endowment, then, sexual intercourse has (and therefore must always retain) a basic procreative orientation.

This point could be reworded in the following way. Availing itself of biological, anthropological, and psychological data, the Catholic position sees human sexuality as a totality. The reproductive orientation of this totality is a basic datum. In this totality nature has provided a human act, a human contribution—sexual

[5] Marc Oraison, *Union in Marital Love* (New York: Macmillan, 1958), p. 3.

intercourse. Rich in essential personal values, this human contribution is neither sufficient for reproduction nor absolute necessary for it. But it is part of a totality which is basically reproductive. The contribution of the human act in this totality: the placement of certain conditions required for the meeting of sperm and ovum. In so far as sexual intercourse does this, it preserves *one* of its basic inner senses within this totality. That is, within the whole structure of the generative endowment, it does what it is supposed to do. It is in this sense alone that copula may be said to have (and must retain) a productive orientation.[6]

But the marital embrace is also essentially an act expressive of personal love. Of its nature it expresses and reinforces the deep personal relationship of unrestricted self-commitment which is the marriage vocation. Because the marriage relationship is one of total mutual self-dedication, the act symbolically expressive of this relationship must be an act of total self-giving. This essential personal character is beginning to receive from theologians the attention it deserves. Only when it does will the moral theology of marital relations be situated at a truly personal level.

In the human context the procreative character of the sexual act is elevated and absorbed into (but not destroyed by) the personal, that is, by the expression of personal love. Thus, as we pointed out, theologians

[6] For an enlightening discussion of this material, cf. Joseph Fuchs, S.J., "Biologie und Ehemoral," *Gregorianum*, 43 (1962), 225-253.

speak of the conjugal embrace as an act of love with a specific procreative character. A fully stated moral analysis of this act will always be at an interpersonal level, at the level of the *Ausdruckshandlung*. It is not as if we had two acts, or a single act with two separable inner senses. The act of intercourse with its double inner sense is one. Because these two characteristics or inner senses fuse in the human context, one may be used as a judgment upon the other. Thus when the procreative potential of the act is defaced, the act will no longer remain *objectively* an act of total self-giving. There will be a restriction, an incompleteness of donation. Similarly when there is *objective* incompleteness of self-donation, this will also be a sign that the procreative chracter of the act has been disturbed.

It is, then, because of the unity of sexual intercourse that the individual inner senses of the act can function as a judgment upon each other. It is quite legitimate to use the procreative "openness" of the human effort as a criterion of its proper performance. This is not biologism. To specify what is meant by complete self-donation is not to descend to mere biology. It is to insist that not just any orgastic experience can be the vehicle of this donation. To choose the procreative capability of the act as a criterion is merely to pick out a single essential aspect of the sexual act and use it as a safeguard for the completeness of union-in-one-flesh. It is to insure the integrity of the expression of love by proscribing possible counterfeits. Does not the refusal to spell out what completeness of giving demands allow nearly any act to be its vehicle? As one

theologian in the preparatory report for the Lambeth
Conference (1958) noted: " 'Relational value' seems
to attach itself to the oddest sexual activities. It is well
known that many people cannot find any satisfaction
at all in the normal act of coitus, but find it in variations
that most would condemn. On what ground are we to
say that these are not pioneers in the development of
the sexual life?"[7]

Catholic teaching insists, then, that to qualify *objectively* as an act of love, the marital embrace must be an
act which is, from the point of view of the human
effort, apt for generation (*apta ad generationem*).
That is, within the totality which is basically reproductive, within the structure of this endowment, it must
do what it is supposed to do—sc., place the act in such
a way that nothing is done to interfere with the meeting of ovum and sperm. It could just as accurately be
stated that to qualify *objectively* as an act of love the
marital embrace must be an act which is an act of
total self-giving (*apta ad amorem exprimendum*). The
procreative criterion is chosen, I would suggest, largely
for pedagogical reasons. It more readily resists the
abuses of interpretation to which the more elusive
term, "complete self-donation," is open. Furthermore,
contraceptive practices, by their very name, force attention on the procreative aspects of the act. It is to be
expected that the rejection of such practices by the

---

[7] *The Family in Contemporary Society*, The Report of a Group
Convened at the Behest of the Archbishop of Canterbury with
Appended Reports from the U.S.A., Canada, and India, S.P.C.K.
(London, 1959), p. 135.

Church would be stated in terms of the challenge
itself.

With increasing emphasis, however, theologians point
out that when there is deliberate interference with the
procreative potential of the act there is *objectively* no
longer an act of personal love. As Joseph Fuchs, S.J.,
remarks:

An act *per se* intimately expressive of personal love is
robbed of its natural *virtus,* if either the method of per-
forming the union expresses some restriction, or the placing of an impediment to conception expresses the exclusion
of the permanent sign of love . . . in either way of acting
there is *per se* expressed a self-donation which is not complete.[8]

With these considerations in mind one can better
understand the difference between periodic continence
and contraception. In the practice of rhythm the sexual
act remains integral, and as such retains its aptitude
for generation and therefore (and above all), its aptitude for the expression of intimate personal love. Con-
trarily, contraceptive acts in some way or other destroy
the aptitude for generation and therefore (and above
all), no longer remain *objectively* expressive of total
self-giving. These reflections lead theologians to the
statement that contraception involves a practical contradiction: the contradiction of willing the act (and
therefore its inner senses) and not willing it (by
rendering it objectively inept to achieve these).

[8] Joseph Fuchs, S.J., *De Castilate et Ordine Sexuali,* privately
printed "Ad Usum Auditorum," Editrice Universita Gregoriana
(Roma, 1959), p. 61.

The distinction between rhythm and contraception can be described, therefore, either in terms of the procreative character of sexual intercourse or in terms of its character as an act expressive of personal love. It is a matter of emphasis. But it is especially from the procreative orientation that traditional principles have judged it possible to clarify the objective incompatibility of conjugal love with contraceptive practices, and sharply to distinguish the latter from periodic continence. In making this distinction Catholic teaching feels that it is not forcing limits on conjugal love, but rather defining its nature and guaranteeing its existence.

Because actual conception is not the sense of this procreative orientation of sexual intercourse and is most often not a possibility, and because marital union is rich in other no less essential (and perhaps even more obvious) values, sexual intercourse will most frequently be sought for reasons other than actual procreation. Indeed this is precisely what occurs in the practice of rhythm. However, since the practice involves avoidance of children through periodic abstention, certain conditions must be fulfilled before the practice is morally acceptable. First of all, both partners must be willing to practice rhythm. For one party to insist on the practice against the reasonable objections of the other would be a violation of a basic marriage commitment. Secondly, both must be able. That is, rhythm must not be the reason for the commission of sins which would not occur without its practice. There are certain obvious dangers in the practice of rhythm which may not be rashly courted. Thirdly, there should be a sufficient reason for the practice, both because of the problems and tensions associated with rhythm and because the best theological opinion admits a positive but limited duty to raise a family. Though there are many interesting and difficult problems touching this duty to procreate, practically it will exist only in so far as it is compatible with the best Christian interests of the individual family; for only then could it promote in any genuine sense the good of the race. If sound principles are properly understood, this aspect of rhythm should not be problematic for the average couple. As Father John Lynch, S.J. writes:

. . . very few of those who bother to seek moral advice on this problem are practicing or contemplating rhythm without reason sufficient to justify their use of it—supposing always willingness and ability on the part of both husband and wife.[9]

Rather it is from the aspect of married love as a vocation to Christian perfection where problems are most likely to be more acute. Sincere Catholics increasingly ask: will our love grow cold if its intimate expressions are regulated by the calendar or thermometer, especially if this becomes a way of life? Is family planning compatible with trust in divine providence? Is it not a selfish preference of our own convenience, a less ascetical way?

There can be no doubt that successful family planning through the practice of rhythm involves a sacrifice of

[9] John Lynch, S.J., in *Theological Studies TS* (1956), 187.

some spontaneity in sexual expression. And this spontaneity is surely an important value. Indeed, its sacrifice may occasion serious tensions, frustrations, distance, mutual irritation and resentment. Man is, however, not merely spontaneity, but (and this, even in the life of conjugal intimacy) spiritually controlled spontaneity. The concrete circumstances of individual couples may compel them to choose between a fully spontaneous sexual expression and observance of the moral order. The inability to realize all abstractly possible values in a given situation is a characteristic human limit.[10] The genuinely human reaction to this limitation is the sacrifice of lesser values to greater.

But the decision to sacrifice lesser values to greater does not guarantee its full success. To be fully fruitful, this sacrifice should not be allowed to remain at the level of a negative, nerve-racking abstention. Indeed, it is quite possibly this negative approach which occasions or at least intensifies the real and often serious consequences of periodic continence. Rather it should be viewed in the fuller context of conjugal chastity. Chastity is necessary for any state of life. Like all virtues, it is a dynamic growth process toward a treasured good, or in the rather static language of the schools, reasonable control in accordance with the ends and purposes of sexuality. As seen by Catholic teaching, marital intimacy is a meeting of *persons*, the loving mutual oblation of *persons* with a specific procreative character. Just as premarital chastity is a

10 Cf. J. Fuchs, S.J., "Geburtenregelung," *Stimmen der Zeit* 170 (1962), 358.

growth process toward the self-possession required to make conjugal intimacy a meeting of persons in mutual self-donation, an integration of love (and therefore freedom) with the sexual, so marital chastity is a continued growth in and deepening of this loving personal exchange. The aim of any couple, then, is to work together toward the ability to make their union an ever more personal experience, hence a matter of loving choice. It is here that many couples will sense the positive values of rhythm. They will confront the (no less painful) demands of rhythm as an opportunity to achieve together the self-possession and control which characterize mature chastity, and therefore as an opportunity to enrich their subsequent relations. They will attempt to convert abstention by necessity into control by choice.

Yet the decision to practice rhythm may bring an indefinable sense of uneasiness, as if the couple were selfishly enjoying their intimacy while deliberately repudiating its essential responsibilities. Unfortunately, this attitude is too often traceable to circles responsible for education to married life. One might usefully distinguish here the decision to limit or space births and actual intimacy under such a decision. If the decision to practice rhythm is sound, there should be little question of selfishness. For marital union is not a mere search for personal pleasure; it is essentially an act of personal communion and mutual self-donation. This inner sense of sexual union is no less essential, and makes no less cogent claims on husband and wife than the procreative sense of intimacy.

Furthermore, the fostering of mutual conjugal love promotes the good of the children in a profound way. Indeed it can be said that education of the child demands a far greater parental closeness than its procreation. It is precisely an underemphasis of these essential personal values of sexuality and their intense interaction on the procreative purposes which can lead to the distorted polarity, "selfish pleasure vs. actual procreation." This is not to deny that selfishness can influence such a decision; it is simply to insist that it need not and should not. In actual intimacy after such a decision, selfishness can be more or less operative as in all human activity. But this is not a quality of rhythm but a reflection of our human condition wherein achievement of mature virtue is a lifetime struggle.

Too often it is said that judicious family planning is not at home with a vigorous trust in divine providence. This may well be a carry-over from times when there was little accurate knowledge about the sterile period and family size was either limited by contraception or left in the hands of God. It may also involve an erroneous mechanistic concept of divine providence. If increased physiological knowledge gives new legitimate capabilities of fertility control, it also enlarges the scope of human decision and responsibility in planning family size.

This does not mean a cessation of divine providence in this area and hence an abdication of reliance on divine providence. It involves at most a change in the manner of this providence. Human reason and ingenuity

are a share in divine providence, and their exercise a
practical way of manifesting trust in God. Failure to
use available legitimate techniques when such use is
prudent is a rejection of means provided by the God
of human reason and as such a practical rejection of
God's providence. But, as Fathers J. C. Ford, S.J., and
Gerald Kelly, S.J., note in their new book:[11]

Reliance on human providence does not mean a calculation
of merely human values, much less mere materialistic ones.
The human providence we speak of is an exercise of
Christian prudence. Responsible parenthood, to be truly
Christian, must put the things of God's supernatural order
in the first place.

The frequency of need for family planning, the difficulties associated with it, and the rich possibilities for
growth through a successful practice of rhythm suggest that knowledge of it (within the context of
Christian chastity) is essential to adequate preparation
for marriage. The problem of family planning is not
met successfully after sexual patterns have settled
deeply and the couple is already crushed under the
burden of its fertility. It must be faced far in advance
both through adequate instruction and gradual buildup
of proper Christian attitudes. There is, then, a duty on
those responsibile for the education of youngsters to
marriage to instruct thoroughly in all aspects of
periodic continence. The medical profession is responsible for the technical aspects, educators and guides,

[11] *Contemporary Moral Theology: Marriage Problems* (West-
minster, Md.: Newman, 1963).

for the moral and spiritual sides. The rhythm system is not a universally applicable or absolutely reliable answer to the problems of fertility; but too frequently its failures can be traced to too little instruction too late. A more organized Catholic effort seems to be imperative, not only to perfect the medical basis for the security of the rhythm method, but also to prepare Catholics for problems involved in its use.

THE PILL

Among family planning procedures rejected by Catholic teaching is the most radical of all contraceptives, direct sterilization. Sterilization is called *direct* by theologians when the impossibility of conception, whether perpetual or temporary, is intended either as an end in itself or as a means to a further end. In other words, it is sterility resulting from an act which *aims at* rendering conception impossible. *Indirect* sterilization, on the contrary, is an unintended by-product of a procedure aimed at some other (than prevention of procreation) purpose. The basic principle upon which Catholic rejection of direct sterilization is founded has been well explained by Denis O'Callaghan.

We have said that direct sterilization is contrary to the natural law and that it cannot be justified by any eugenic or therapeutic expediency. On the other hand, we know that direct mutilation of the ordinary organs of the body is justifiable in certain circumstances, namely, when the good of the whole person demands the removal of an organ or the suppression of a function. So, for example, a surgeon may remove a gangrenous foot, a man trapped by the hand in a burning vehicle may cut off the limb in order to escape. But a surgeon, even with the highest motives, may not sterilize a woman in order to avoid the danger of pregnancy and childbirth.

What marks off the generative function from the other functions of the body? What distinguishes sterilization from simple mutilation? The answer is that sterilization adds a new dimension to simple mutilation. The individual organs of the body are immediately ordained to the good of the whole person; they are so absorbed by the whole that they possess no finality or purpose independent of the person. The generative function, however, has a finality of its own in that it is primarily directed to the good of the species rather than to the good of the individual. Consequently, since one must take account of this innate purpose, the principles governing its suppression are more complex than those for simple mutilation.[12]

The reproductive capacity has a basic primary finality which transcends the individual; hence, direct disposition of this capacity is subject to definite limits. The apparent naturalness of temporary direct sterilization by steroid hormones has failed to shake the conviction of theologians that this application is incompatible with man's limited rights over his physical integrity.

This is the *basic* principle according to which direct sterilization is rejected. Sterilization is a word like contraception; that is, verbally it focuses on a physiological phenomenon. It is quite natural, therefore, that the principles basic to the rejection of direct

[12] *Moral Principles of Fertility Control* (Dublin: Clonmore and Reynolds, Ltd., 1960), pp. 17-18.

sterilization should begin at this level. It is my opinion, however, that to be fully adequate to the human situation, the rejection of sterilization must eventually reach the level of interpersonal relations. This can be achieved only, it would seem, if it is shown that direct sterilization affects the sexual act as an act expressive of personal love. It is precisely this that Joseph Fuchs, S.J., has attempted to do in showing that direct sterilization impairs the sexual act as an act of complete self-donation. This conclusion, of course, is much more subtle and elusive, much more difficult of the type of rational demonstration which we have (erroneously, I believe) been expected to make in this area. It is extremely difficult to *prove* anything about human love. But is this not all the more reason why an age which has not been enviably successful in the management of its sexual life should sense the value of further guidance—especially when that guidance emanates from an authority which has received a divine commission and the promise of divine support in the execution of this commission?

While the character of human sexuality yields the conclusion that direct sterilization is immoral, nevertheless the reproductive organs are parts of the body and as such share the subordination to the whole which is characteristic of a part. Hence, under carefully specified conditions, most theologians have tentatively endorsed the use of hormone drugs for genuinely therapeutic uses (even though incidentally sterilizing) —among them attempts at regularization of the female ovulatory cycle to allow for a successful practice of periodic continence. I say "tentatively" for at least two reasons. First of all, the legitimate application of the principle of two effects demands, as one of its conditions, a proportion between the evil permitted and the good to be anticipated. Until the long range side-effects of progestational therapy are known (the matter is still debated in medical circles), this proportion cannot be accurately computed. Hence any application of the principle of double effect must be hypothetical, or tentative. Secondly (with regard to regularization of the female cycle), moralists assume

on the authority of certain doctors who have proposed the treatment as medically feasible, that the regularity of ovulation eventually to be achieved is not due causally to the temporary period of sterility which also occurs in the patient, but is rather the immediate effect of the restoration of hormonal balance which the medication achieves. Temporary sterility, in other words, is not the directly intended means whereby regularity of ovulation is accomplished, but rather an indirect by-product of therapy whose direct result is regularization of the ovulatory cycle."[13]

If this assumption should be undermined by further medical investigation, a different moral analysis would have to be made.

The fact that the steroid pills do not directly affect the generative act itself but rather the generative faculty, the fact that their effect is temporary and reversible, some popular confusion attributable to several factors, plus the subtlety of the matter, inevitably raises the question: to what extent is the question of the present

[13] John J. Lynch, S.J., in *Theological Studies*, 23 (1962), 244.

pill still open? The question might be more precisely worded: to what extent are the following statements "open questions"? (1) Non-punitive direct sterilization (even temporary) is intrinsically immoral. (2) Contraceptive use of hormonal drugs is direct sterilization.

A detailed answer to this question is impossible. It would suppose a clairvoyance beyond the claims of ordinary men. That is, it would suppose a precise appreciation of the shortcomings of our present understanding of direct sterilization plus a pre-cognition of future developments likely to refine our knowledge. It would be far more acceptable to offer some general considerations which would make our continual reassessment of our present position an intelligent and prudent procedure.

First of all, the term "open question" is vague and can mean at least several things: (1) capable of being reversed; (2) capable of being challenged theoretically, either as to conclusion or method of argumentation; (3) capable of being nuanced; (4) capable of being rejected at the practical level. Before concluding to what degree the question of the pill is an "open question," the precise sense of this term should be made clear.

Secondly, the position whose openness is under discussion should be carefully distinguished in terms of the authority with which the position is proposed and its actual theological status. In terms of formal proposal by the Church, there seems to be a degree of clarity on several points. (1) The rejection of direct sterilization in general (including temporary sterilization) and most especially of the sterilizing use of the pill in particular is proposed with considerably less solemnity than the teaching on contraception. (2) Rejection of contraceptive sterilization pertains to the authentic but non-infallible teaching of the Church. (3) Such propositions are *zeitverbunden* and hence not only allow but demand continued theological revaluation. (4) One can frequently distinguish the conclusion from the argumentation used to establish it. (5) The effect of such a proposition is, in varying degrees, a presumption of certainty which does not, however, forbid prudent investigation, discussion, and publication. As for the actual theological status of the two statements, they seem to be in the category of practical certainties.

Thirdly, traditional principles seem committed to the procreative character of individual acts. This has been a long tradition in Catholic theology, is clearly the partial basis for contemporary authentic rejection of contraception and contraceptive sterilization, and is the unanimous (hitherto) position of theological writings.

Finally, in assessing the openness of the two statements, professional discussants will wish to consider the relevance of the following two points: (1) definitions are rarely static; (2) clarity of definition or principle need not imply clarity of application. Practical situations have refined and are capable of refining even further our understanding of direct sterilization.

Yet, consider more specifically the relevance of the following practical situations: (*a*) the case of suppression of presumably abnormal fertility (e.g., during the post-partum months); (b) the case of defense (through temporary sterilization) against the probable effects of rape; (c) the famous case of the badly scarred uterus after repeated caesarean section. (In connection with this last case and others analogous to it, there has come to my attention recently a considerable body of Continental theological opinion which would like to narrow the definition of direct sterilization to the prevention of *procreation*—in the fullest human sense— as contrasted with prevention of mere *conception*.) These cases and their nuances can be found thoroughly discussed in professional theological literature. It would be beyond my purpose to present these discussions here. But it is important to note that to some extent or other such situations subject the standard definition of direct sterilization to the need of refinement.

In light of these general considerations only one innocent of history, theology, and human limitations will contend that present formulations are exhaustive of the truth and that the question on the pill is in every sense a closed question.

Birth Control, Abortion, Sterilization, and Public Policy

JOHN E. DUNSFORD

A growing organized effort to revise public policy on contraceptive birth control is crystallizing both on the domestic scene, where the burdens of providing welfare payments to the needy and socially disadvantaged are creating enormous tax bills, and on the international, where the burgeoning world population is evoking pervasive fears for the success of foreign aid programs and future life on the planet. Increasingly, Catholic individuals and organizations will be challenged to take public stands on a host of questions growing out of the population problem. Not only to avoid inconsistencies from one issue to another, but primarily so that Catholics can discharge intelligently and wisely their duties as citizens, guidelines for decisions on these major social problems are imperative.

If the Catholic community wishes to partcipate in the shaping of public policy on these issues, however, it must initially clarify any articulate more precisely than has yet been done the Catholic philosophy on family limitation. Traditional teaching on the subject must be given modern relevance, and must be cleansed of the encrusted folklore of the past which hides or distorts the central meaning of the Catholic position on sex, conception, and family size. Until Catholics are clear about the exact contours of their views on the goal of family planning, in a degree approaching their firmness of opinion regarding contraceptive means, they cannot confidently engage in public debate of complex legal and political matters.

GENERAL PREMISES

What should be the public policy in the United States in regard to contraceptive birth control? The question must be considered not as an exercise on the morality of law in a vacuum, but with regard to the concrete and particular circumstances of American society today. As St. Thomas said, "Laws imposed on men should also be in keeping with their condition, . . . law should be possible both according to nature, and according to the customs of the country."

For the Catholic, the matter cannot be one purely of political expediency, for presumably there are limits both to what he can personally accept as valid legislation and to what he wishes to impose on other persons as a legal requirement. At the same time, the Catholic recognizes that the challenge of erecting a viable public policy demands a thorough knowledge of the political conditions under which the law will be received.

Certain premises provide a frame of reference for this short discussion of the posture which Catholics might adopt on this legal and public issue. The first is that the immorality of an action is not in and of itself a necessary or sufficient reason for prohibition by the instrument of civil law. The diffidence in seizing on legislation to promote morality, reflected in the premise, derives not only from the practical consideration of extreme difficulty in enforcing such laws (e.g., a prohibition against lying), nor even from the apprehension of greater evils which may result from the implementation of some laws (e.g., the possibility of corruption of public officials or general lawlessness under a Volstead Act), but also from an awareness that the sphere of concern for the state is a limited one (e.g., imposition of a religious belief on citizens would represent a violation of the individual conscience).

A second premise relates to the social imperative that the law maintain a prudent awareness of the public morality, for the requirements of the law must be realizable in a given milieu and time. This premise grows out of the experience that a law which is not observed or respected may breed a contempt or disrespect for the legal order which is disproportionate to anything achieved by the specific regulation itself. The art of government consists as much in knowing when not, as when to legislate.

Still another premise, however, recognizes that law does exert power to lead and educate men in the ordering of their lives. Law is more than the common denominator of society since it provides the context in which individual standards of right and wrong are oriented and structured. Under some circumstances, a duty would exist to oppose and disobey civil law which was unjust. And affirmatively, the citizen should work for laws which promote the common good.

In a pluralistic society, ideological groups—whether religious in character or not—cannot expect to force their convictions or beliefs upon others. At the same time, such groups have a claim to the maximum possible accommodations to pursue their own ends consistent with the common good. This is not to say that the conception of the common good must be devoid of any form of ideology. In some instances, a common consensus may be found between the major groups of the society making for a tolerable agreement. And the opportunity must always be kept open for one group through zealous persuasion to convince the community that a particular ideal should be embraced and embodied in law. Great problems emerge, however, when groups with conflicting beliefs maintain that the common good requires that their particular commitment be endorsed and promoted by the state.

In the United States the Catholic community is the primary force which refuses to accept the methods of contraceptive birth control. The degree to which most Americans employ such devices would indicate that possibly a majority in this country either find no moral problem in such usage or do not have sufficient strong beliefs in the matter to prohibit their use. Finally, a smaller portion of the population seems to insist that under the present circumstances, considering the success of the various forms of limiting births, there may be a moral obligation to employ contraceptive birth control.

THE STATUS QUO

Catholics may opt to maintain the status quo which, though in practice it does not materially impede the use of contraceptives, at least formally restricts the employment of controls which are objectionable to them (see appendix). Bishop Karl J. Alter has stated well the historical irony of present Protestant insistence on repealing the old laws on the books, pointing out:

Various Protestant churches at the time (of the passage of these laws) were definitely opposed to the dissemination of such information. It was under their influence, or at least with their approval, that the prohibitory laws were placed on the statute books.

Yet any realistic appraisal of the present currents of action and thought casts considerable doubt that a policy of maintaining the existing legal structure can be anything more than a delaying action. Modern conceptions of the role of spouse, the growing burdens of state welfare programs on national resources and economy, the international concern over the growing world population—all supply impetus to the forces of change. Writing on the political economy of population growth, one non-Catholic commentator is convinced of one conclusion:

More control, principally through governmental programs, is inevitable. The only question is whether it is to be de-

veloped with at least attempted rationality and with due
regard to the preservation of democratic values, or whether
affairs will be allowed to drift into conditions approaching authoritarianism.[1]

The suggestion of authoritarian measures is not mis-
placed, when one considers that a bill was introduced
in the Mississippi State Senate in 1962 which would
have required mothers on welfare rolls who gave birth
to an illegitimate child to attend a planned parenthood
clinic or be held guilty of a misdemeanor.[2] If Catholics
should choose to stand on existing public policy, they
must consider the fact that social forces too long
bottled up will sometimes explode in extreme and un-
predictable ways.

On the assumption, then, that some affirmative response to the social ferment on the birth control issue
is called for, it may be instructive to consider several
distinct objects of public regulation: (1) the use of
contraceptive birth control devices; (2) the availability
and dissemination of these devices; (3) governmental
inducement to employ these devices.

THE USE OF CONTRACEPTIVES

Attempts to ban the use of contraceptives by individuals, even in a society which takes a common and
condemnatory view of their morality, creates problems

[1] Arthur S. Miller, "Some Observations on the Political Economy of Population Growth," 25 *Law and Contemporary Problems*, 623.
[2] Committee Substitute for Senate Bill No. 1984, introduced by
Senators Montgomery and Williams.

of enforcement which are intolerable. From the nature of the relationship and the act in which the immoral device is used, the legal intrusion tends to destroy important values of individual integrity, family autonomy, and rights of privacy. Connecticut appears to be the only state which presently has such a law. Despite the fact that it is ineffective, the very presence of the statute is a constant source of irritation to many non-Catholics and a basis for charges that a Catholic political bloc has no scruples about restricting the personal freedoms of other citizens when it has the votes to do so. Succinctly stated, the arguments against such a law are that it is incapable of enforcement, it represents an unjustified extension of state control over essentially private acts, and it breeds contempt for the processes of law themselves. If these indictments of law pertaining to use of contraceptives are valid—and it would seem that many of the objections would apply to the prohibition of use by the unmarried as well as the married—then a Catholic approach to public policy in this area might affirmatively oppose the existence of such legislation. The disengagement from the status quo would have to be accomplished in a way that left no doubt of the moral evil of individual resort to contraceptives.

SALE AND DISSEMINATION OF CONTRACEPTIVES

The legal regulation of the sale and advertising of contraceptives is quite another matter from the viewpoint of feasibility and the integrity of the civil law. The prevailing law on the subject, as a result of exceptions written into the statutes, court interpretations and enforcement, does not seriously impede individual acquisition of contraceptive devices. A policy judgment based exclusively on Catholic standards might point to the need for the state to prohibit the manufacture and sale of these instruments of immoral purpose. In fact, the likelihood of such an eventuality is nil, since one would expect that any modifications or revisions of the statutes will be in the direction of making the law more reflective of community attitudes about the acceptability of contraceptives. Confronted by that probability, Catholics must make a basic decision about the role they want to play in the formation of public policy.

On one hand, Catholics may decide to serve a prophetic mission, manifesting their commitment to the demands of the Natural Law by opposing any form of permissiveness on the part of the state in regard to these devices. Such a position would logically call for the repudiation of the present set of laws, most of which make exceptions to the restrictions on sale and distribution of contraceptives. In those states where no laws presently exist, attempts might be made to secure legislation of a prohibitory character. A range of policy choices would be open, however, and *ad hoc* determinations could be made from one situation to another as how best to oppose legal acceptance of these devices. Exclusively from the viewpoint of the Catholic as citizen, this approach can be justified as a fulfillment of the important function of dissent in a democracy. By repeatedly raising his voice in opposition to toleration of such practices, the Catholic could pay his society the great service of exerting whatever force he has against a type of commerce which is detrimental to the moral fiber of the nation.

But there are also great disadvantages to this approach. In all likelihood, a cost would be paid in terms of the non-Catholic's estimation of the Church as an institution. Catholics might very well be condemned as callous, or contemptuous of the political rights of others (though any prohibitory law to some extent limits individual freedom). Furthermore, the effectiveness of Catholic participation in the formulation of public policy may be materially reduced if the emerging consensus focuses on the question of how the laws are to be loosened. If Catholics content themselves with sweeping rejection of any permissiveness, they are not likely to contribute much to the particular changes that seem inevitable.

Catholics might choose to play a different public role in the anticipated reformation of present law on the sale and dissemination of artificial birth control devices. As far as the state's toleration of such devices, the Catholic might conclude that under existing conditions the demands of pluralism and civil peace require that the law be permitted to acknowledge in form what it now accepts in fact, the civic rights of those married couples who think these devices legitimate to have an unimpeded access to them. This conclusion would take into consideration the cultural conditioning and moral ignorance of many Americans on these matters. Such a policy would not be based on the impropriety of legal action in this area, nor would it counsel an abandonment of all regulation of contraceptives. To the contrary, it might permit Catholics to assist in the formulation of new laws which provide more adequate assurance that contraceptives are not readily available to minors, or unmarried persons, or whatever groups would be judged by a strong public consensus inappropriate for voluntary decision in this matter. If there is a significant body of Protestant opinion which genuinely feels a moral duty to employ contraceptives, this approach would make an accommodation in terms of their religious liberty. From a practical standpoint, greater legal permissiveness on contraceptives may be preferable to the prospect of legislation encouraging sterilization and abortion. And in the given context of American society, filled with erotic stimuli and fostering easy marriage, legal prohibition of contraceptives—if effective—may be productive of more harm than good.

But there are grave difficulties in this approach, too. Catholics may be deemed to approve or condone artificial birth control, when in effect the advocacy of such a policy only relates to the complex of factors which indicates that more restrictive legal action is socially unwise. Another consideration is the effect which such a policy, even assuming it can be formulated in a clear and adequate fashion, would have on the Catholic community itself in terms of its awareness of the immorality of the use of contraceptives.

Finally, it should be recognized that once changes are embodied in the law they may remain there indefinitely—indeed, the inertia of the law is reflected in the fact that present laws have proven impervious to the radical revision of popular thinking on contraceptives. Just as divorce statutes have become firmly embedded in the body of American law, breeding numerous problems as the years pass, so might legislation of greater permissiveness on artificial birth control not only entrench itself but gradually enlarge the range of its effects.

STATE INVOLVEMENT

Since in actual practice the law offers little resistance to the acquisition of contraceptives by those who desire them, the pressure to rewrite state statutes is apparently not as great as is the current effort to involve public agencies such as hospitals and welfare boards in the promotion, or provision, of these devices. In contrast to state permissiveness on the matter of private individuals buying and using artificial birth-control instruments, or in permitting private physicians to prescribe such methods for medical or general health reasons, what is now being urged increasingly is action by the state to provide services for birth control to those persons coming within the coverage of public health and welfare agencies. The form of the programs will differ from locale to locale; referrals to planned parenthood clinics may be proposed, or instruction by public service nurses, or counseling by doctors in public hospitals, or free provisions of the devices themselves. In several Southern states, such programs have been in operation for years, and in some municipal areas doctors may prescribe forms of artificial birth control for medical and health reasons.

While this type of state involvement is analytically distinct from mere permissiveness on the part of the state regarding the actions of private individuals, it represents a predictable extension of the concept of state neutrality on such matters. The argument for such programs is very simple: if persons of private means are enabled to take advantage of contraceptives and effective family planning, why should not the same opportunity be provided to those who have no moral scruples about such means but either are ignorant of their existence or financially unable to afford proper instruction and the instrument itself. These programs are not rendered less attractive to many Americans by the promise they hold out of reducing the cost of public medical care, tax-supported programs of aid to dependent children, and so on. By a curious quirk of fate, the idealistic humanitarian and the hard-bitten taxpayer find themselves pulling in the same direction.

The particularly objectionable feature of such arrangements to the Catholic is the deployment of official energies and public funds to measures which are intrinsically immoral. A claim can be made that the state abandons neutrality on the issue when it participates in the utilization of artificial birth controls by its citizens. Neutrality is thus conceived in terms of the state remaining aloof from the question and cutting off all connections with committed private groups in the society. An analogy might be drawn to the judicial interpretation of the establishment clause of the First Amendment, under which church and state are theoretically separated by a wall. If the state cannot properly acknowledge religious institutions or attempt to treat them impartially, so the argument might run, then neither should it affiliate (even in the most impartial way) with any program that runs counter to the moral beliefs of a substantial portion of its citizenry. The argument need not be a narrow legal one, but rather based on broader principles of political justice and equity.

Should Catholics choose to pursue this analysis, however, they must be prepared to explain how they distinguish the birth control situation from that of claims for support of their own parochial schools. For in fact most Catholics do not find the rigorous separatist theory of church-state compatible with their viewpoint of a just society. The Catholic community believes that a genuine state neutrality in the area of education would require the state to make a *pro rata* contribution to that portion of church-sponsored education which serves a secular need. Generally, it is not the Catholic who demands that neutrality be defined in terms of complete divorcement of all religious elements from the public area. Of course, the objectives of education and those of artificial birth control are quite different; for his own purposes the Catholic finds no difficulty in saying that the state should support the one and oppose the other. But the basis of such a distinction is a code of morality which many non-Catholic Americans do not share, or a reading of the Natural Law which others are blind to. In the political and legal arena, the Catholic's ultimate argument for his right to share in public educational benefits is that the state ought not to disqualify training under religious auspices and thus prefer the secular. Neutrality here is defined not in terms of the state keeping completely free from the subject, but rather in terms of state impartiality. Why, then, should not those persons desiring birth-control help have state aid available to them as long as it is provided in an impartial manner, neither demanding that persons employ such measures nor prohibiting them from doing so?

STATE NEUTRALITY

In a theoretic analysis, it could be said that when the state and its agents merely respond to the demands of a part of the population, they are not urging any particular course of action but merely statically reflecting the voluntary choices of citizens. The further point is sometimes made that no one is required to accept such services, that doctors and nurses whose conscience will not permit participation in these affairs may be excused. In the practical realm, however, the initiation and implementation of these programs often represent something more than mere state neutrality.

In the first place, the desire to incorporate counseling and referrals into the state welfare and health programs stems in some part from the experience that the work of voluntary agencies in promoting contraceptive birth control is relatively ineffective. In a recent pamphlet of the Planned Parenthood Federation, the point is made several times that women are more often inclined to adopt such measures when the service is provided at the hospital at the time of a birth, or where counseling is done in the home rather than at a central locale to which the woman must travel. In other words, the convenience and success of the program are probably materially aided by the state's involvement. Secondly, the actual implementation of these programs creates significant obstacles to a genuine neutrality, even assuming the best of intentions on the part of all concerned. How much time and trouble will be taken to determine the moral acceptability of these means to particular patients? Who will make the inquiry of the patient? How does the reliance of the patient on the doctor or nurse influence the choice which allegedly is a free one of the individual? A recital of the program in the Denver General Hospital is provocative of questions which this type of state service creates:

Two regular postpartum clinics are held weekly. A nurse from the Planned Parenthood group briefly interviews each patient after she has registered, to determine if she is interested in contraceptive advice. Methods available are briefly described and the patient expresses her preference.

The patient then receives her regular postpartum examination from the physician and he prescribes the method to be used. He follows the patient's preferences where possible, but changes them where there is a medical reason for doing so. All of the presently accepted contraceptive methods are available, including the pill and rhythm. The nurse from Planned Parenthood then sees the patient again and instructs her in detail in the use of the chosen contraceptive method.

The hospital furnishes room and a small cabinet for storage of supplies. There is no cost to the City (although many feel it would be a perfectly legitimate use of public funds to finance this program, just as it is being done in the tax-supported hospitals in New York City). We regard this arrangement as a useful first step toward a full and comprehensive birth-control service, offered by the hospital in exactly the same manner that it offers other medical services. . . .

The most important statistic is that, of these women who were accepting contraceptive help 89 per cent had never been seen previously by the Denver Planned Parenthood Clinic. The addition of family planning services to our clinic did not merely shift patients from one facility to another; it actually reached an entirely new group.[3]

On the assumption that the Catholic community should adopt a policy of state neutrality on the matter of contraceptive birth control, it is apparent that enormous practical problems of achieving a true neutrality exist. It may be that in this area, as the Supreme Court seems to conclude regarding prayer in public schools, there is no workable compromise in a public institution that will provide a satisfactory protection for all ideological interests. Once again the analogy is offered with caution, for the question of

[3] William Goddard, M.D., "Denver: Experience in a Public Hospital," *Birth Control Services*.

state promotion of birth control is not legally a First Amendment problem of establishing a religion. Perhaps it can be raised as an aspect of the freedom of religion clause if pressures are brought on individuals in these programs to violate their religious beliefs. In this connection, it must be remembered that the philosophic dilemma of modern Church-State law is the seeming disadvantage which it imposes on religious action in contrast to the freedom of all other ideological commitments.

Particularly in the field of public health and welfare, where the individual clients may often be malleable and peculiarly subject to the suggestions of state agents seeking to help them, the form of the service provided by the state will be determinative of whether actual promotion and inducement of the use of these means is employed. A complicating element inherent in the choice of programs is the prescription of these devices by many doctors as part of the medical treatment of the patient, or the recommendation of such devices as part of the social worker's professional assistance. How can the hazards of *de facto* promotion of contraceptive birth control be separated from the full range of other professional services?

In considering the private citizen's use of contraceptive birth control, and the public sale and dissemination of these devices, both the capacity of the individual to make a judgment for himself and the financial ability to implement this judgment were assumed. In the area of public health and welfare, however, both of those elements may assume different dimensions. Some members of the public welfare population may have neither the initiative nor the desire to undertake the use of birth limitation measures, whether morally licit or not. While the person unquestionably can make a legally binding decision on the matter, he or she is relatively uneducated to the significance or meaning of that judgment. Similarly, even though the cost of a preferred manner of family limitation (through licit or illicit means) may be negligible, the individual involved is operating on a minimum subsistence.

Operating public clinics where the indigent and disadvantaged may resort for advice and help in effectuating private decisions is in legal principle quite close to the decision to accept a permissiveness in these matters. The clinics would in effect be removing economic and social obstacles to equality of moral and personal decision. Once having decided that the state, from reasons of sound politics and effective law, should stay neutral on the matter of contraceptives, the clinics themselves might be abided. From this perspective the crucial fact would not be the expenditure of state funds to provide the counseling or cost of birth control, but the influence and pressure which might be brought directly or indirectly by the state to persuade individuals to adopt such measures. If the state engaged in extensive advertising and recommendation of clinics, for example, it would no longer be neutral. On the other hand, a state-sponsored campaign to encourage people to think seriously about family limitation in the light of their moral commitments might or might not be objectionable, depending upon the Catholic specification of conviction on that matter.

In actual operation, however, the decision to provide counseling and birth control devices is not isolated from other governmental functions. State involvement in the matter has come out of the programs of aid for medical and welfare purposes. As a result, both the public health doctor and the state social worker may be precipitating influences in the individual decision to resort to contraceptive birth control. The most intractable aspects of achieving a neutrality on these means are found in the structure of the professional relationships created.

A number of variations in the structure of welfare programs suggest themselves. Two extreme positions in the range of possible choices that might be put into practice are (1) to prohibit any mention of, prescription for, or reference to birth control measures by public officials in welfare programs; (2) to compel the individual beneficiaries to conform to decisions by state agents about their sexual habits. The first position, which many Catholics may wish to see as the prevailing one, seems unrealistic in view of the attitude most Americans have about these devices. The second position, which Catholics would of course resist vigorously, is totalitarian by nearly any standard. If one were to assume that state doctors and social workers will incorporate counseling concerning artificial birth control in their professional care (due allowance being made for the conscience of Catholics in these positions), and further assume that the state will in some respects finance not only the counseling but the use of the instruments for avoidance of conception, the problem of keeping the state impartial on the matter of whether contraceptive birth control is chosen still remains. At a minimum, some provision would have to be made to raise the question of the morality of these means for the individual welfare client. This could be done by the professional worker during the course of processing a case, but it is at least doubtful that a doctor or social worker who routinely advocates contraceptives will be solicitous and patient enough to permit the client the full deliberation that should go into such a decision. For that reason, it might be desirable to separate the counseling function from the servicing function, that is, to require the actual instruction and provision of the devices to come from a private agency, or from a distinct state agency, only upon the initiative of the individual welfare client. Whether the state paid the private agency or not, or whether the state provided its own clinics or not, this procedure would require the individual person to indicate by his action in accepting the referral and making proper application to the designated agency that he is freely choosing these means. To some extent the hazard of the individual being swept up in the irresistable efficiency of a singly-administered state program is avoided.

If the separation of counseling from servicing is deemed too nice a refinement in the execution of these programs, it might alternatively be required that those who are the object of state concern be made accessible to interested private agencies prior to the individual decision as to whether or not to accept the birth control means. For instance, the name of a welfare recipient might be referred to the appropriate religious denomination if one has been designated. If this is considered improper under existing theories of State-Church separation, then at least the religious agencies might be given opportunity to check public records systematically with the purpose of seeking out and discussing the matter with the individuals involved. When a Planned Parenthood nurse is stationed in a hospital, as in the Denver example mentioned above, it seems reasonable to permit equal access to patients by religious bodies. Such a procedure to be successful would obviously require a good deal of organization and manpower on the part of the religious bodies themselves.

APPENDIX

EXISTING LAW AND PUBLIC POLICY ON BIRTH
CONTROL, STERILIZATION AND ABORTION

Superficial reading of the law on the books would
suggest that both the federal government and the
majority of states strictly regulate and generally restrict
the promotion, mailing, sale and advertisement of
contraceptives. In addition to the Federal law (18
U.S.C., sec. 1461-62; Tariff Act of 1930, 46 Stat. 688,
19 U.S.C., sec. 1305) some 34 states (as of 1960) have
enacted some form of birth control legislation (cita-
tions to state laws may be found at 70 *Yale Law
Journal*, 322, 333, Appendix A). But it is a fact of
common experience in the American environment that
the form of these laws does not reflect accurately the
attitude of the population toward the legitimacy of the
use of contraceptives generally or the circumstances
under which resort to such devices is justifiable.

Recognition of the shifting American convictions on
these matters has led Federal courts to imply a limitation on the Federal statute which sweepingly bans the
mailing of contraceptives and printed matter on their
use. An intention to use the devices for illegal purposes
has been held essential to conviction under the law,

John E. Dunsford 107

with the result that druggists, jobbers and physicians are entitled to receive them (St. John-Stevas, "Birth Control and Public Policy," pp. 16-19).

A recent summary of state laws listed 20 states and the District of Columbia as having no regulation on dissemination of birth control information; 17 with laws prohibiting use or distribution except to doctors, pharamacists, etc; five with prohibitions against sale or distribution to anyone; one with prohibition against use, and two with prohibition of establishment of birth control clinics.

A gradual unraveling of the public consensus on birth control has been occurring since 1873, the date of the passage of the Comstock law by Congress. When most of the birth-control laws were passed in the United States after the Civil War, the American people by and large agreed that there were grave social and moral dangers associated with contraceptive devices. Radical changes in the attitude of many religious bodies have substantially altered this picture. The sociological studies on the prevalence of contraceptives in American marriages indicate that the legal formulations of the last hundred years are rapidly being drained of their power to guide human action in this regard. So empty of significance are some of these laws that the Supreme Court of the United States dismissed a Connecticut case two years ago by pointing out that only one prosecution had been initiated in three-quarters of a century. This particular law prohibited the use of contraceptives, but even the information representing the single exception to 75 years of official lethargy was itself dismissed by the State after a favorable judicial ruling on the constitutionality of the statute. This state law was characterized by Justice Frankfurter as "harmless, empty shadows" (Poe v. Ullmann, 367 U.S. 497).

This is not to say, however, that all of the existing laws are necessarily dead letters. Obviously, the enforcement effort may differ from state to state (or in a given state, from election to election). But more important, the laws have assumed a variety of forms which introduce correspondingly different considerations in an evaluation of their social effect as well as their relevance to contemporary mores.

A simplified categorization of the legal posture taken by states on the matter might be constructed, as follows:

1. No law at all.

2. A prohibition of advertisements.

3. A prohibition on the sale and/or advertising of contraceptives, with exceptions for physicians and sometimes pharmacists to distribute them for medical reasons, and exceptions for advertisements in medical journals and the like.

4. A prohibition on sales to unmarried persons and from slot machines.

5. A prohibition of sale and advertising.

6. A prohibition on use as well as sale and advertising. In discussing the Connecticut law prohibiting the use of contraceptives, Justice Douglas considered some elements for judicial consideration in weighing the constitutionality of birth control restrictions:

John E. Dunsford

If a State banned completely the sale of contraceptives in drug stores, the case would be quite different. It might seem to some or to all judges an unreasonable restriction. Yet it might not be irrational to conclude that a better way of dispensing these articles is through physicians. The same might be said of a state law banning the manufacture of contraceptives. Health, religious and moral arguments might be marshalled pro and con. Yet it is not for judges to weigh the evidence. When either the sale or the manufacture are put under regulation, the strictures are on business and commercial dealings that have had a long history with the police power of the States. . . . The regulation in this case touches the relationship between man and wife. It reaches into the intimacies of the marriage relationship. If we imagine a regime of full enforcement of the law in the manner of an Anthony Comstock, we should reach the point where search warrants issued and officers appeared in bedrooms to find out what went on. . . . That is an invasion of the privacy that is implicit in a free society (81 S.Ct. 1765) (dissenting opinion).

This statement is not offered as an authoritative exposition of the constitutionality of various birth control laws, although an educated opinion would be that prohibition of the use of contraceptives by married couples violates the due process clause of the Fourteenth Amendment. (Indeed, this was the position taken by the only two Justices who reached the merits in the Poe v. Ullmann decision.) The Douglas dicta, however, is worthy of serious consideration in what it tells us about the significance of the means employed by a state to achieve a particular regulatory end. In a broader perspective, it seems clear that many persons o legal restrictions upon contraceptives generally would be equally opposed to unrestricted access to the devices by the young and unmarried. The point is that while the existing laws no longer express a clear American consensus on the morality or aesthetics or desirability of contraceptives, the probabilities are that most people accept the need for some kind of regulation of the devices. Distinctions are drawn by many between contraceptive birth control in special cases such as serious danger to the health of the mother, in family planning as a personal decision of the husband and wife, in illicit sexual relationships to avoid pregnancies, in state-sponsored programs designed to reduce the relief rolls.

Oddly enough, the bases for some of these distinctions have already been explicitly utilized in framing existing laws on abortion and sterilization. The oddity appears in the fact that the popular attitude toward these two methods of controlling family size and population is, in all likelihood, nowhere as favorable as it is toward the use of contraceptives.

While it is true that nearly every state makes the procurement or attempted procurement of abortion a felony, exceptions are commonly written into these laws permitting the act to preserve the life of the mother, or her health. (See "Criminal Abortion: Human Hardship and Unyielding Laws," 35 S. Calif. 123,127.) In practice, these exceptions are liberally applied and abortions often performed in violation of the law (Ibid., p. 126). Thus, in terms of the Catholic community, the present laws on abortion admit of practices which are morally condemned. And while the movement to enlarge the area of legally permissible abortion is perhaps not as insistent a social force as is the birth control groups, signs already point quite clearly to a growing trend in this direction. The number of illegal abortions, sometimes estimated as high as one out of five pregnancies totaling some one million operations a year, is raising questions about the adequacy of the present statutes.

Sterilization statutes are found in 28 states, in 23 of which the operation is compulsory for persons with certain forms of physical and mental defects. The remainder of the 28 have procedures for consent of the person, or a combination of permissive and compulsory procedures (St. John-Stevas, *Life, Death and the Law,* Appendix IX). In all of the states prior to 1962 the purpose of the legislation was eugenic or therapeutic and the operation covered only defective persons, howsoever defined. In that year, however, the state of Virginia passed a law which permits the sterilization of any person who has the consent of the spouse, receives a full explanation of the consequences from a doctor, and waits for thirty days (H.B. No. 300, 1962 Acts, Chapter 45, Appendix A; "The Virginia Voluntary Sterilization Act of 1962," 13 Social Order 38, 1963). By merely expressing the desire and fulfilling the conditions listed, a person in Virginia may choose sterilization for whatever reasons he deems proper. (Aside from statutes dealing with sterilization, the legality of the operation on a private, voluntary basis is quite ambiguous.)

As of today, then, the public policy in this country on artificial birth control, abortion, and sterilization is either in practice (nonenforcement of statutes against the dissemination of contraceptives) or in legal effect (exceptions to the sale of contraceptives, aborting of foetuses, and sterilizing of defectives) in conflict with the Catholic morality that forbids these practices no matter what the social or personal reason. Yet the present policy is merely permissive for the most part. Except for eugenic sterilization, the state does not compel the individual to submit to any of these methods of fertility and life control; at least in theory the state is committed in fact to restrictions upon these practices. The Virginia statute on sterilization may portend a more active State role in the entire area, either through greater permissiveness or through involvement in programs which will *de facto* promote the employment of these methods for other than medical or eugenic ends.

Natural Law and Contraception

FREDERICK J. CROSSON

The inseparability of human existence and Natural Law is as clear today as it ever was. They are wedded together, and this marriage was indeed "made in heaven." There are those who would like to effect a divorce; there are those who praise Natural Law inordinately, and expect too much of her; and there are those who realize that any marriage involves collisions, adjustments, and development on both sides.

Without ultimately relying on Natural Law, we could never speak of human *development* but only of *process*; we could never reasonably sanction any action, whether by praise or blame, reward or penalty; there would be no purpose in discussing or deliberating about a choice between various satisfactions of our needs; we could not assert the inhumanity of cannibalism or genocide. This may sound as if I am praising Natural Law inordinately, but really all I have said so far is that we would not be human apart from her: I have not commended her, but rather the marriage. If

the organization of society and of individual lives is
not founded on arbitrary decision which is "against
common right and reason," as Coke declared—then
there are guideposts, norms, by which we can take our
bearings.

Why not rest with arbitrary decision? Why not define
justice as whatever the legislature allows, define law
as "the prophecies of what the courts will do in fact,
and nothing more pretentious"? Many books have
been written to answer this question. I can only indicate here two kinds of response, one direct, the other
indirect or dialectical. The first would be an appeal to
the facts: all powerful men or groups *do* have a
natural inclination, feel an obligation, to assure themselves of, and have public recognition of, the legitimacy of their position and the reasonableness of their
decisions. The second response would be to uncover
the normative presuppositions of such definitions as
that of Holmes (quoted above): What is a court?
Could a group of children constiute a court? Does it
have to give reasons for its decisions?

Is it not, however, true that no such objective order of
norms has been found? Is it not true that history and
anthropology discover to us "an indefinite variety of
notions of right or justice"? This now classic objection
of historical and cultural relativitism has, I think, had
its fangs drawn in recent years. It still has some teeth,
and some are still sharp, but most of them have been
seen to be blunted on closer examination. My own view
parallels that of Professor Leo Strauss:[1] "One cannot

[1] *Natural Right and History* (Chicago: University of Chicago
Press, 1953), pp. 9-10.

understand the meaning of the attack on natural right in the name of history [and anthropology] before one has realized the utter irrelevance of this argument." "(P)recisely if natural right is rational, its discovery presupposes the cultivation of reason, and therefore natural right will not be known universally," i.e., conceptually known and institutionally embodied in the same ways. In other words, by arguing that there is no form of justice that has not been denied somewhere or at some time, "one has not yet proved that any given denial was justified or reasonable."

Furthermore, "Knowledge of the indefinitely large variety of notions about right and wrong is so far from being incompatible with the idea of natural right that it is the essential condition for the emergence of that idea: realization of the variety of notions of right is *the* incentive for the quest for natural right."

That is, it is precisely the conflict of customs that motivates a reflection on the notion of custom, on "our" way of doing things, and a splitting of that notion into two parts: nature and convention, or nature and art. Some of our customs are of human invention, man-made, and some are natural, the "right way," and are only discovered or discerned by man.

Both nature and art are generative or dynamic principles for Aristotle: their only difference is that nature is built *into* things—it is the root of their *typical* mode of functioning—while art is employed *on* things, and makes them change or develop in a non-natural way. Thus, animals are born with certain instinctive reactions, but they can also be conditioned by an experimenter to react in a certain way. Or, a tree naturally grows into a certain typical shape, but it will never shape itself into a table without the art of the carpenter.

Put in this way, art seems to be an interference with nature; it redirects or changes altogether the normal path of functioning. This is the sense in which *artificial* birth control is said to be wrong. But art need not do this: as a distinct principle of formation it may merely assist the natural process by removing impediments to natural functioning, as the farmer waters the dry land or the physician extricates a bullet. "Art partly completes nature, partly it imitates nature," Aristotle says.[2] It would certainly be wrong to oppose the two flatly and unqualifiedly.

However when we come to man, the problem becomes more complicated. Let us set it up by juxtaposing two texts of Aquinas. On the one hand, in discussing matrimony, he says "Nature intends not merely the generation of the offspring, but also . . . its development . . . to the state of virtue."[3] On the other hand, he says that the virtues do not arise in us by nature.[4] This makes it look as if nature "intends" something which by its own dynamism it is incapable of achieving. Aquinas is here following Aristotle, who says[5] that none of the moral virtues is engendered in us by nature (ψύσει), nor is any engendered contrary to nature (παρὰ ψύσιν).[6] We are apt to receive them, but

[2] *Physics* 199 a 16.
[3] Sum. Theol. Suppl. 41, 1.
[4] I-II, 51, 1; 63, 1.
[5] *Ethics* 1103 a 18.
[6] *Ibid.*, 1103 a 24.

we do not naturally acquire them. This means that unlike the role of art in farming and medicine, there can be no question here of art merely removing impediments or providing the proper conditions for natural development. Art, human invention, must here play a positive and intrinsic role, and not a merely conditional one.

We can reformulate this by distinguishing three kinds of potentiality in things. (I run the risk here of seeming pedantic, but the point is important.) There is first the *natural potentiality* of anything, its capability and inclination to become or develop in a typical way, provided it is not impeded. Second, there is what I might call *"artificial potentiality,"* a passive capacity to be worked on. Aquinas does not use this term, because, as he says, "The production of artificial things is not natural, because although there is a material principle in that which comes to be, it does not have a natural potency for such a form."[7] Third, there is, peculiar to man, what I shall call *human potentiality:* the real capacity in the child to become fully human, but *without* an efficacious inclination.

Man is, therefore, as a mature creature the product of both art and nature (or history and nature, as a modern would say)—and this not in the banal sense that part of his development is natural and part "environmental" or conventional, but rather that his development is through and through a dialectical exchange of these two. If we are to bring nature (i.e., what is natural) to birth, the midwifery of art is indispensable.

[7] In *II Phys.* 1.

If we can get an obstetrician, so much the better, but most societies have had to get by with midwives.

Nature, said Heraclitus, loves to hide. Human nature hides in the indefinitely large variety of notions of good and bad. The problem is not whether nature is, i.e., whether there are inclinations; the problem is that of their specification. All are inclined to act justly. The problem is, e.g., is slavery just? How do we find out? Note that the question could not be asked until slavery existed. Note also that the answer is not self-evident: we cannot rely on people's intuition to tell them that slavery is wrong. The recognition, the knowledge *that* it is wrong took time and reflection to acquire. When it is seen to be wrong, then the inclination to do what is right will slowly assert itself.

By what does art guide itself in forming the humanity of man? (My terminology here is derived from Cicero's remark that while we are born men, we are not born human.) The modern historicist or relativist, who identifies nature with process, will say with R. G. Collingwood[8] that man's "nature" is simply what man does and has done in history. Collingwood characterizes the modern view by saying that it views the "fabric of human society [as] created by man out of nothing."[9] This is simply the counterpart to a naive interpretation of the classical view, which sees human nature asserting itself in vegetable fashion, and of course tends to identify the conventions of "our society" with those of nature.

[8] *The Idea of History* (Oxford: the Clarendon Press, 1946), pp. 10, 229.
[9] *Ibid.*, p. 42.

But we cannot be guided simply by a knowledge of man's essence, i.e., by the definition of man as a rational animal. For aside from the fact that primitive societies do not know such a definition, man's essence is what is already given at the origin of development. It is the *perfection* of the rational animal that is problematic. When Aristotle seeks to draw some guidelines for *praxis* from the notion of man's nature,[10] he can get only quite general ones: that man's good lies in the virtuous exercise of his faculties, i.e., an exercise directed by right reason.

The thesis presented here then is that the decisions about organizing society and forming one's character *must* involve a certain amount of experiential probing and indeed experimental creativity. (The analogy of the fine arts is suggestive: the poet or painter indeed begins with some idea of what he wants to make, but it is not a fully-formed idea, pre-existing its embodiment. Nevertheless, it is sufficiently definite that the poet knows when to erase a line, the painter when to amplify line and color.) This is why not only wide experience is necessary, but also time: more time apparently than the classical formulators of the doctrine realized. Indeed some scholastic philosophers argue that some of man's natural inclinations can be manifested only after long centuries of preparation.[11] This is *one* of the major reasons for the variability of notions of right and wrong.

There are, as Aquinas noted, several other reasons.

[10] *Ethics* I.
[11] E.g., Jacques Maritain, *Man and the State* (Chicago: University of Chicago Press, 1951), p. 94.

Ignorance of the secondary or proximate principles of natural law is one; variability of circumstances is another. Thus the inclination to be just did not yet exclude torture as a judicial instrument in Elizabethan England; and thus the obligation to restore goods held in trust need not always be observed.[12]

To account for this diversity, once the doctrine is assured, is not difficult; the real problem, of course, is eliciting the natural or normative from the diversity of phenomena. (The expositions of Aquinas and many manuals tend to by-pass this problem because they are theological in form.) No search for "cultural universals" will, of itself, yield natural law norms (the "naturalistic fallacy"). What is required in the crucial area of the epistemology of natural law is a "reading" of the facts, a discrimination which is guided by, but not determined by, what happens for the most part. Once we pass beyond the most obvious and primordial instantiations of the Decalogue, one cannot rely on immediate intellectual insight, as was noted earlier. Reason, ratiocination must come into play and exercise a critical function. Yet again, this is not immediately sufficient: it suffices to mention the critical justifications of slavery and torture, and the condemnation of usury.

We can locate the problem in the context of the classical theory by asking how the process of concretion is to be construed: how are the more proximate and specific principles derived from the more general ones? Jacques Maritain has contended that they are not de-

[12] *Sum. Theol.* I-II, 94, 4.

duced, but are known by inclination, by a kind of
perception of the congenial character of certain
actions. That is, they are not *arrived at* by conceptual
analysis but by a connatural insight. But insights and
intuitions, however invaluable and indispensable, are
like the wisdom of the majority: at any given moment,
it may be a false wisdom, and only time and analysis
will *manifest* the correctness of the judgment.

(This may be the reason for what is, from one aspect,
a frustrating facet of Aquinas' expositions of natural
law. He never gives, as examples of Natural Law
judgments, any but those which have been recognized
for centuries. His analysis is retrospective, not pro-
spective, and tends thus to certify the status quo. But it
may be that his avoiding of new extensions is deliberate, and that our modern haste to extend the
mantle of Natural Law over a great variety of novel
phenomena is imprudently precipitate.)[13]

I would prefer to speak of an intuitive induction, in
Aristotle's sense: not one based on statistical sampling,
but one which grasps the *meaning* which unites a set
of previously disparate or unconnected phenomena, or
assimilates to a unified set a series of actions previously unrelated to them. The model for this kind of
seeing is provided by the Gestalt analysis of perception. It involves a selection of the relevant elements
of the object or objects regarded, and a relegation of
the other elements to the background. Within such a
focal area, ratiocination, deduction, analysis become

[13] Cf. Robert Hutchins' catalogue in *Natural Law and Modern
Society* (Cleveland: World, 1963), pp. 36-37.

meaningful and well-founded. But it is possible, as John Wisdom has remarked, to have all the elements of a pattern before you and still to miss the pattern.

The notion of a pattern suggests why the "facts" are necessary to such cognition, but not determinative by themselves. On the other hand, once the pattern is seen, it is difficult to recall or realize how the facts looked before. We today find it difficult or impossible to understand how torture could have been tolerated as a judicial method for so long. The process of cumulative insight is irreversible, and this is as true for science and art as it is for morality.

This topic—that of the "logic of discovery" in Natural Law—requires far more attention than it has yet received. As Father Murray has remarked, "The theory of Natural Law has not been adequately developed so that you can put the bite on many of the situations that confront us today." It seems to me that the problem is not so much development as method of development: *how* is it developed?

I can pursue this no further in the time allowed, but I would like to finish this section by quoting a philosopher of science, Michael Polanyi, whose theory of knowledge is rich in implications for Natural Law. I think that the application here will be clear.

. . . any critical verification of a scientific statement requires the same powers for recognizing rationality in nature as does the process of scientific discovery, even though it exercises these at a lower level. When philosophers analyse the verification of scientific laws, they invariably choose as specimens such laws as are not in doubt, and thus inevitably overlook the intervention of these powers. They are describing the practical demonstration of scientific law, and not its critical verification. As a result we are given an account of the scientific method which, having left out the process of discovery on the grounds that it follows no definite method, overlooks the process of verification as well, by referring only to examples where no real verification takes place.[14]

II

Aquinas capsulizes the schema of natural law[15] in terms of three intrinsic inclinations in man, which have been summed up as self-preservation, self-propagation, and self-fulfillment through intellectual and moral virtue. The first two of these he pairs off neatly with food (or nutrition) and sex (or reproduction), following Augustine as well as Aristotle. Augustine's statement, which he quotes,[16] is "what food is to the welfare of a man, such is sexual intercourse to the welfare of the whole human race." The Aristotelian root of this is the doctrine that living beings attempt to imitate the Prime Mover's eternity by insuring the eternity of the species through reproduction.[17]

This principle of the bio-social character of intercourse is the bedrock foundation of the Catholic tradition. It is a firm foundation, but it has proven to be too narrow. Aquinas makes it the center of his discussion

[14] Michael Polanyi, *Personal Knowledge* (Chicago: University of Chicago Press, 1958), pp. 13-14.
[15] *Sum. Theol.*, I-II, 94, 2.
[16] *Ibid.*, II-II, 153, 2.
[17] *De Anima*, 415 b 1-8.

of all questions relating to the use of venereal acts. From it he concludes to the wrongness of concubinage, sodomy, fornication, incest, and so on.

Thus the only argument that he offers against fornication (assuming that it is not compounded by being adulterous, incestuous, etc.) is that the unstable union militates against the welfare of the (possible) children. He assumes that the result of intercourse is or may be —and not just *ought* to be—procreation.

The limited character of his position appears clearly if we press him on a crucial point, the relation of *individual* actions under the food-sex analogy. The purpose of eating is nutrition, but this does not prevent an occasional non-nutritive use of the faculty of ingestion and digestion. Why then must every copulative act be regulated by the general purpose of the faculty? Aquinas replies to such an objection:

One copulation may result in the begetting of a man, wherefore inordinate copulation, which hinders the good of the future child, is a motal sin as to the very genus of the act, and not only as to the inordinateness of concupiscence. On the other hand, one meal does not hinder the good of a man's whole life, wherefore the act of gluttony is not a mortal sin by reason of its genus. It would, however, be a mortal sin, if a man were knowingly to partake of a food which would alter the whole condition of his life.[18]

Clearly, in the face of modern techniques, or even before the question of a perfect contraceptive in principle, this position needs to be extended. It *was* ex-

[18] *Sum. Theol.*, II-II, 154, 2, 6m.

Frederick J. Crosson

tended by emphasizing the *normative* character of the function. Its essential purpose is generation, and, to quote Aquinas again, it is sinful if "the seed be emitted in such a way that generation cannot ensue."[19] Of course, he immediately qualifies this by saying that such acts are licit if generation is only accidentally prevented, e.g., in the case of sterility.

But this so-called "perverted faculty" argument, although stated on such a level as to apply to every instance of intercourse, seems to encounter the opposite problem, namely to prove too much. Thus there appear to be exceptions to almost every such general maxim where circumstances change the "moral species" of the act: e.g., saying the opposite of what is in one's mind, or taking another's life.

More pertinently, it appears to go against the concession made by Aquinas above, namely, that so long as the *general* function of the faculty is fulfilled, individual divergencies are at least not mortal sins.

To buttress this argument, various *ex consequentia* arguments have been adduced, but their value depends on whether or not the consequences are *essentially entailed* (for the most part) by the action. Aquinas was perfectly willing to argue from experience if it were "proper accidents" which were revealed (e.g., he argues thus for monogamy and private property).

The difficulty with resting the argument on the bio-social teleology of the act, then, seems to be that while it will determine the morality of the function in general, it does not appear to determine individual acts in

[19] *Sum. Contra Gentiles*, III, 122; cf. *Sum. Theol.*, II-II, 154, 1c.

a firm and decisive way, *provided that* these acts are within the context of general fulfillment. If I am not mistaken, this would constitute the point of assimilation of rhythm into the classical doctrine. As Father Thomas put it, it is (not the individual act, but) "the process of sexual relations which is procreative."

But of course new problems arise immediately. For once we have admitted that the individual act need not provide even the possibility of procreation *so long as it is in the context* of general fulfillment, the question arises, what do we mean by "in the context"? What norms still guide the secondary or relational end of the function? What still belongs to the "integrity of the act" when it is not *immediately* determined by the procreative function? In particular, is the integrity of the act violated by the use of some or all contraceptives?

If we are guided by the food analogy, we might ask first in what sense the consumption of non-nutritive substances must be in the context of nutrition. Note that we would not and could not ask this question except insofar as we are dealing with the same kind of act (i.e., eating). The exception tests the rule only insofar as it is an instance of the rule. This suggests that "in the context" entails that the same kind of act is thus justified. In the case of the sex act, this is the same act which is socially and morally validated by the institution of marriage. Otherwise, why justify the act only within marriage? Why not remit the wrongness of fornication, especially when the partners are in love?

"In the context" means that the procreative act remains paradigmatic. It is difficult to see how, if this criterion is abandoned—as it was by the Lambeth Conference of 1958, in opposition to the Lambeth Conferences of 1908, 1920 and 1930—any moral limitation can be placed on the relational employment of venereal acts, provided only that they are (in the words of the Lambeth statement) "mutually acceptable to husband and wife in Christian conscience." This abandonment constitutes a refusal to assist authoritatively in the formation of the Christian conscience, a refusal which is, admittedly, one persistent element in the Protestant tradition.

But now, precisely *what* is paradigmatic in that act? Here we face the final specification of the concrete, the critical point at which current opinion divides so sharply.

I want to say that the act is *not* paradigmatic because it is generative, but rather that it is generative and paradigmatic because it is an act of love, indeed the primordial act of love. In saying this, I invoke a tradition which goes back beyond Christianity and finds its first philosophical analysis in Plato's *Symposium*. In the course of criticizing homosexuality, Plato points out that love is not merely the love of the good and the beautiful, but of generation and birth in beauty,[20] whether of body or of soul.

We touch here on a point which is muted in Aquinas' discussions, oriented as they are by the bio-social aspect of marriage. I mean, of course, the interpersonal

[20] *Symp. 206.*

aspect. The slighting of this aspect has adverse reper-
cussions elsewhere in Aquinas' theory, notably in the
weakness of his arguments for the indissolubility of
marriage.

(Let me remark in passing that discussions of the
"personalist" dimension of marriage all too often verge
on or become superficial and sentimental. The reason
for this is generally the lack of a carefully laid ontology
of intersubjectivity: a precise treatment of the real,
ontological differences through which personal existence develops. At the same time, it must be recognized
that invoking "personalism" does not automatically
make all things new and better. Charity today is
no more vital simply because our spirituality is
more personally oriented. The fact that "togetherness"
could rapidly become a derisive epithet speaks for
itself.)

As an act of love, then, the conjugal act is *unitive* and
it is a *gift*. These, I suggest, are its invariant elements
as a paradigm.

It is *unitive* because it unites man and wife, and here
the physical union is necessary to but not sufficient
for any further union. It is unitive because the physical
union founds and sustains a passage from object to
subject, from "exterior" to "interior," or, if you like,
from body to soul. I once heard a beautiful woman say
that she liked to look "sexy" but she didn't like to be
treated "sexy." If this is a paradox, it is a profoundly
human one. Aquinas touches on this in justifying
sexual relations merely for pleasure: this is licit, he

says, provided that it is as a wife and not as a woman that a man treats his wife.[21] The act is unitive also as *expressing* union—no couple can have *human* intercourse immediately after an argument, say, while not speaking to each other—and as *nurturing* union, for it draws them into a personal intimacy which they will share until death, in spite of any separation.

The act is a *gift* because every deliberate human action, an *a fortiori* every interpersonal action, has a human meaning. The human meaning of the conjugal act, the transmission of seed from man to woman, is only weakly expressed in the agent-patient analysis. The sense in which marriage as a whole, and in particular the conjugal act, is a gift is a sense far less present to consciousness than the unitive aspect. I mean, it is present on a deeper level. It comes out, as Freud comments, in talk about man and wife complementing each other, each having something to offer which the other does not have.

Fundamentally it is the gift of self, as we say. But of course the self is not anything we *have* which we can hand over, it is what we *are*. Self-giving is absolutely dependent on giving of non-self, i.e., of other things. We give ourselves *in* the *manner* in which we give other things. Conversely, we can give ourselves in the manner in which we accept. As Gabriel Marcel has noted,

A gift, whatever it may be, is never purely and simply *received* by a subject who has nothing to do but make a

[21] *Sum. Theol. Suppl.*, 49, 6.

place for it in himself. The truth is much rather that the gift is a call to which we have to make a response.[22]

That is, the ability to give is conditioned by an attitude of receptivity, of *welcome* on the part of the receiver. The "gift" that arrives in the mail from Lever Brothers or the Colgate company is called so only by the faintest of metaphorical extensions, in spite of the letter that accompanies it.

The question now is, to what extent must acts which are relational in intent, but "justified by the context," i.e., by the social, physical and moral relations of the partners, exemplify these invariants? Can we say that such acts must include the transmission of *verum semen* in the uterus? It would seem that we can, if indeed as an act of love the marital act is generative, as was argued.

Of course, other relational acts which contribute to the completion of the paradigmatic act are not excluded by this conclusion. The licitness of such secondary acts will involve considerations of esthetics, personal taste and cultural mores. It will also involve considering whether such acts enter into the paradigm class, i.e., bring into play those physical organs whose heterosexual employment defines what we have called the "context." The claim here is that if they do enter into the context, and do not exemplify the invariants of the paradigm, then they are illicit, morally and socially.

Everything turns here on *seeing*, and there is no deny-

[22] *Homo Viator*, tr. Emma Crawfurd (Chicago: Regnery, 1951), p. 62.

ing that many do not see the necessity, even some who defend Natural Law. But it is no argument against the necessity that many do not see it. Such deficiency is present on every level of human cognition, from sense experience to theoretical implications of a principle. There *is* a danger of seeing what we are habituated to see, or want to see. The only protection against that danger is discussion, a discussion in which each tries to say not only what he sees, but also tries to say why the other does not see.

An Integrated Outline of Conference Principles

DONALD N. BARRETT

Little is more flattering to a reader or auditor than to be addressed by an expert as a colleague. In what follows, however, we attempt to adduce some summary principles raised by individual experts without laying claim to co-equal status in the field of morals. Recognition is given that many assumptions concerning our knowledge are generously made by the experts in terms of Church teaching and Christian philosophy. Thus, a serious responsibility attaches itself to those who seek to wrestle with these questions.

In a similar vein the present précis must be cast within the restricted frame established for the discussions. No question is raised implicitly or explicitly about the formal and official teachings of the Church, but in the mode of Thomas Aquinas, *ex eis (haec doctrina) procedit ad aliquid aliud ostendendum*. By open discussion arguments are formulated to deepen and broaden our knowledge and appreciation of Church teaching.

A new catechism of simple questions and answers cannot be found here, either in intention or execution.

Various perspectives are explored and there is no design to make final judgment on crucial issues which are still "open." The following statements are intended merely to bring together from the several papers and discussion an orderly outline of the ideas presented.

MORAL ISSUES AND
THE POPULATION QUESTION

I. THE SETTING

A. EMPIRICAL SITUATIONS DEMANDING SOLUTIONS:

1. the population explosion has a shocking aspect for the whole world, especially for those nations with a greater responsibility;

   (Häring, p. 4; Thomas, p. 42; *et al.*)

2. families have changed significantly since our moral outlook and principles were developed— they are smaller, move more often, marry younger, live together longer, have more material goods, expect more from marriage.

   (Imbiorski, discussion abstract)

3. millions of Catholics do not understand and/or appreciate the Church's doctrine on sexuality; we may be losing great numbers;

   (*Ibid.*)

4. spontaneity in sexuality is often correctly expected, and abstinence, rhythm do not always meet the needs;

   (*Ibid.*)

5. a legalistic or canonical approach does not face the need, especially in terms of live and religious elements in marriage;

(*Ibid.*)

6. policies concerning sexual questions in countless cities and in the nation are now being formed, and the urgency of our participation cannot expect pure negativism, nor can it wait for slow change in our moral perspectives;

(*Ibid.*; Dunsford, pp. 85-90; *et al.*)

7. existing laws regarding abortion, birth control and sterilization are undergoing extensive revision and pressure for revision is felt. What are proper Catholic policies;

(Dunsford, appendix, pp. 106-112)

8. English Catholics have family counselling centers, approved by hierarchy, financed by local governments, in which counsel is given by laymen (doctors trained), not clergy, on the medical, spiritual and social aspects of marriage; why not in U.S.;

(Shuster, Jacobson notes)

9. Catholic priests are giving very different responses on morals of rhythm and sexuality; also laity differ greatly, as evidenced by large numbers of indignant responses to articles by Fr. Thomas and Fr. O'Brien;

(O'Brien, Jacobson notes)

B. RESPONSE TO NEEDS:

1. Vatican Council II is a positive and pastoral response to these problems; the general pastoral

response must emphasize the conjugal act itself
and its biological performance;

(Häring, p. 1)

2. the doctrine of the Catholic Church on married
life I do not think will be changed in basic
principle, but it can be better integrated into the
great commandment of love and the law of
growth—a dynamic, pastoral and foreseeing
approach;

(Häring, pp. 17-18)

3. we must here analyze both the changing and the
changeless aspects of the teachings of the
Church;

(Kerns, p. 23)

4. the present problems are non-postponable, and
we must face up to them now;

(Thomas, Jacobson notes)

5. we must face the problems, yet avoid the
dangers of mistake and error;

(Crosson, pp. 130-131)

C. DEVELOPMENT IN THEOLOGY:

1. I and many others think there is great progress
in moral theology and official Church doctrine
in rethinking and reformulating such problems; example of responsible parenthood;

(Häring, p. 4)

2. the history of moral theology . . . proves that
there is genuine development of doctrine, possibilities of better integration, better arguments
and necessary distinctions; Catholics do not

think they have resolved all problems in the
sexual area;

(Häring, p. 22)

3. we forget that professional theologians were
historically arguing issues on sexuality among
themselves, and that the laity ignored most of
it and their practice was moral; this dialogue
between the theologian and the layman in the
development of theological principles must not
be forgotten;

(Kerns, p. 27, *et passim*)

4. moral and pastoral theology have to consider
sociological, cultural and ecumenical back-
grounds of the principles formed earlier and
reconsider them in view of the present situation;

(Häring, p. 4)

5. theologians need sociological research, not
merely as useful to its function, but necessary
to it; we must watch the signs of the times;
without psychological and sociological research
we cannot speak to men of today; research
could show us much;

(Häring, pp. 6-7)

6. the Catholic community of the United States
must find a way of cooperating with their fel-
low citizens in dealing with the population explosion;

(O'Brien, Jacobson notes)

7. cooperation with other Christians and non-
Christians on many levels is clearly indicated to
Catholics;

(Häring, p. 2)

8. research by Catholics themselves is badly needed on many fronts; Catholic moralists often do not know reality in terms of the specialists in biological and social sciences; lack of empirical knowledge has led moralists to defective interpretations of natural law. We have too easy recourse to traditional formularies (presumed knowledge of natural law and the Church), whereas we should start with a broad spectrum of hypotheses; separately and together moralists and social-biological scientists strive for an ever more realistic basis for Catholic policy, so that we may touch and influence the modern conscience in accordance with our obligation and mandate—this must be done in an atmosphere of free inquiry not purely on the basis of authority or assumed status;

some problems needing research: a) how does the coming of the third and fourth child influence the first and second; b) if trained medical doctors give spiritual as well as medical advice in the counselling centers in England, with Church approval, why not in the United States; c) if rhythm is espoused openly in England by Catholic agencies, why not in the U.S.; d) if in England there is open cooperation with birth control agencies, why not in the U.S.; e) if the "pill" was not opposed by Church authority in Santiago, Chile, why is it opposed in the United States; f) how do we teach responsible parenthood to everyone; g) what precisely is responsible parenthood; h) how can we best organize the pastoral efforts of the Church in regard to Marriage and Sexuality; *i*) how, at what age, where should sex education be given to youth, since we know that it does not work effectively now according to current methods; *j*) what are the important distinctions between the "private" and "public" conscience in our need to participate in the formation of public policy in regard to sexuality; *k*) what are the sociological barriers to implementation of a policy by the Church in different communities which are being pushed into contraceptive and other programs; *l*) how actually effective are rhythm and various forms of contraception (not in laboratories but in actuality in solving family and community problems, e.g. rising numbers on relief).

(Discussion, précis, *passim*)

II. RESPONSIBLE PARENTHOOD

A. MATRIMONY AND MARRIAGE:

1. Chastity is the virtue that regulates the use of sex in conformity with right reason (a form of temperance); reasoning from the origin, nature, destiny of man, and purposes of his reproductive system, theologians conclude that the venereal pleasure must be avoided by the unmarried and must be regulated by the married according to the ends of marriage and the purposes of the generative act;

(Thomas, p. 52)

2. all persons are gravely obliged to strive towards full chastity . . .; completely free and deliberate

acts to the contrary are to be considered mortal sins. Such acts are not always mortal sins, however;

(Häring, pp. 15-16)

3. the Church condemns artificial insemination even within marriage (as a substitute for natural intercourse) and stresses that the conjugal act is far more than an organic function;

(McCormick, p. 62)

4. the bio-social character of intercourse is the basic principle of Catholic tradition and Aquinas makes it the center of all issues regarding venereal acts; yet Aquinas had a very narrow conception of the principle of procreation, not noting that many conjugal acts are non-procreative (just as some eating is non-nutritive in purpose);

(Crosson, pp. 123-124)

5. regarding matrimony, Aquinas says that nature intends not merely the generation of offspring, but also its development to the state of virtue; this requires outside influence and art;

(Crosson, pp. 116-117)

6. of course, the basic natural law principle says: what is essentially against nature can never and for no reason be justified as morally good—as given in *Casti Connubii*; but this is not biological only;

(Häring, pp. 11-12)

B. PROBLEMS OF ENDS:

1. the objective ends of marriage: as there is a dual sexual nature of man (male-female), there is also a double finality (parenthood and mutual

fulfillment), as indicated in Genesis; the couple
seeks mutual fulfillment through dedication to
God's service and the special mission of procreation and education of children;

(Thomas, pp. 52-53)

2. to say that the large family is the Catholic ideal
   is a dangerous oversimplification; the Church
   insists that there are excusing causes "in truth
   very wide" from such an objective;

(McCormick, p. 61)

3. a heavy emphasis is placed on personal values
   in marriage (for the partners) by authentic
   Catholic teaching, and further the Church insists that procreation and *education* must go
   together;

(McCormick, p. 61)

4. procreation-education is the "primary" end of
   marriage in the meaning that it is the specifying
   end, distinguishing marriage from all other
   types of association, partnership, etc. between
   man and woman (brother-sister, father-daughter); only marriage puts the couple in a "procreative status" for acts apt by their nature for
   begetting children;

(Thomas, pp. 54-55)

5. "primary" and "secondary" refer to *objective*
   ends (inherent in the structure of marriage),
   showing that the secondary is objectively designed to make the primary more easily and
   adequately achieved; thus, sexual relations are
   secondary in the sense that they must be used
   unselfishly to strengthen the union and fulfill
   their roles as partners and parents;

(Thomas, p. 55)

6. "primary" end does not mean that the couple should have as many children as they are biologically able, since each couple differs in capacity to fulfill parenthood-education;

(Thomas, p. 56)

7. conjugal love, as secondary end, is far more than what some theologians call mutual help; more and more theologians consider married love not a goal or end but *causa formalis* of marriage as a sacrament; in proper order the couple goes to the altar already in love (not afterwards) and also because they want to have children; love and procreation are in the same order of causality; it is a most dangerous error against psychological reality and the very essence of the sacrament to consider married love in a dangerous competition with procreation and education; we must stress conjugal love, the necessity of marital love's cultivation, which is the source of parental love;

(Häring, pp. 7-8)

8. emphasis on the right biological performance of the act remains at the level of mere animals; there must be continuous effort to grow in love;

(Häring, p. 10)

9. earlier theologians' lack of knowledge of the total procreational function and other factors accounts for the quasi-fixation on the procreational function, and their unrealistic readiness to recommend absolute abstinence over long periods, their justification of rhythm's use as more or less a concession to fallen nature and in general their devaluation of the relational, personalist function in love;

(Thomas, pp. 49-50)

10. sex in its individual aspect operates on at least three levels: the psycho-sexual (genital), psycho-social (masculinity-femininity), and spiritual (transcendental and supernatural); it must be understood and judged accordingly;

(Thomas, p. 46)

11. since each act of intercourse does not procreate, we could say that the "process of sexual relations" is procreative; in procreativity the relational-personalist-love elements are integrally involved;

(Thomas, p. 49)

12. unselfish love is beginning to receive from theologians the attention it deserves; when procreativity or self-donation is incomplete, then the other end of the act is objectively restricted, i.e., each end serves as a judgment on the other; this ensures the integrity of procreative love, the unity of sexual intercourse;

(McCormick, p. 68)

13. moralists and pastoralists differ significantly in their explanations of ends of marriage; some seem to create a "doctrinal imbalance" by emphasizing what should not be done and not stating what should positively be done;

(Discussion abstract)

14. the "personalist" approach to the ends of marriage stresses the moral determination of human acts by way of the inter-personal relations involved, i.e., of the couple, parent-child, person-God; the obligation to develop and act as a full person (in the philosophic sense) serves to demark the moral principles applicable in human acts; without confrontation with the

personal-other there is no morality in such acts,
i.e., at least with a personal God (or at most);
(Johann, Jacobson notes)

15. contrary to the personalist approach the argument is made that the procreation-education approach gives a clear norm for judging morality
of acts, whereas the personalist leaves too much
vague and defined by a non-analyzable "love";
(Thomas, Jacobson notes)

C. NORMATIVE AND RESPONSIBLE PARENTHOOD:

1. first consideration must be given to responsible
parenthood, but the concept must be purified;
today it often means something with no eternal
values considered, or it means a way of keeping one's present standard of living;
(Häring, p. 2)

2. in Catholic morality responsible parenthood
means giving a generous response to the challenging gifts of God; more specifically it means
the judgment whether another child is desirable
now—not a judgment made once for all time;
it must be an authentic image of the religious
and moral life of those who make it, showing
growth in sanctity, generosity:
(Häring, p. 3)

3. no one can make the judgment as to what responsible parenthood means for a specific
couple other than the married couple themselves;
(Häring, pp. 2-3)

4. therefore, for one family it may mean only one

child, and for another it may mean one beyond the tenth child; they must consider such things as health, home conditions, educational facilities, and many other "very wide" circumstances, within the context of generosity and sanctity;

(Häring, p. 3)

5. it would be wrong to impose high heroism on all without respect for the law of growth and without preparation for this heroism in the whole Christian life; responsibility and realism are also needed;

(Häring, p. 3)

6. the quantity of children (many or few) neither implies nor precludes quality, happiness and sanctification of family members, their well-being and growth in love;

(McCormick, p. 63)

7. it is not true that judicious family planning is not at home with a vigorous trust in divine providence; our increased physiological knowledge enlarges the scope of human decision and responsibility in legitimate fertility control; human reason is a share in divine providence and exercising it manifests trust in God; failure to use legitimate techniques when it is prudent rejects His providence in a practical way;

(McCormick, p. 76)

8. the need for family planning, its difficulties and its rich possibilities for growth suggest that knowledge of it is essential to adequate preparation for marriage; it must be faced far in advance through adequate instruction and the building of Christian attitudes; youngsters must

be so instructed; medical men and educators must be involved; failure of rhythm is more often the result of instruction too little and too late, in the moral, social and medical spheres;

(McCormick, p. 77)

9. two phases in the development of counselling were stressed: *a*) the great need for training in counselling for all clergy, in order to mitigate the scandal which is being given them in advising couples in ways revealing tremendous misunderstanding of moral and social principles, e.g., this was recognized in England and medico-moral-pastoral conferences are now common; *b*) the need to work with non-Catholics in counselling; the need for the professional help of the laity; the family, school, pulpit and individual counselling in regard to sex is not working; non-Catholics are sincere and consider their sex values moral; they are ahead of us in reaching the laity in counselling and we must learn from them, e.g., we must not look upon rhythm as an emergency solution to a problem.

one conference participant on the second day said it would be imprudent to advise a couple not to have children today, although many others objected and said it can be recommended in view of the great poverty of over two-thirds of the world and millions in the United States; this participant went further to say that only when rhythm becomes effectively reliable can the question of moral responsibility to have or not have children be taken up; on the third day he insisted that we must talk of the *virtue* of rhythm, a positive good to be encouraged and cultivated;

(Discussion, précis, *passim*)

D. LOVE AND THE CONJUGAL ACT:

1. the first and noblest obligation in married life is the unselfish giving of oneself and grateful acceptance of the giving of the other; striving to this ideal is genuine love;

(Häring, p. 10)

2. placing chief emphasis on the biological factor not only neglects the very essence of the sacrament as a supernatural covenant of love, but also neglects the actual context of psychological and social needs, e.g., exclusiveness of married love is lessened if they do not cultivate conjugal love, in a society where frequent contact of the sexes is the standard;

(Häring, p. 10)

3. the Greek Fathers and many in the West had to struggle against the old pagan gloom, seeing matter as evil and marriage as a sin; Christ's presence at Cana should settle any doubts as to what God thinks of marriage; God is the one responsible for it and it is part of His design;

(Kerns, pp. 24-26)

4. but what is the design, a concession to human weakness? The Church has never given the considered view that marriage is a sin, nor the result of sin; but since the writings of Augustine, the sex instinct (not marriage) seems traced to original sin; sexual intercourse is per-

mitted only because of offspring, fidelity and the sacred pledge;

(Kerns, pp. 26-27)

5. by the sixteenth century intercourse is considered blameless only if the motive prompting it is one of the end of marriage; but this motive may be *virtual*; Pius XII said the couple does no wrong in seeking enjoyment this way, since they accept thereby what the creator has designed for them;

(Kerns, pp. 29-34)

6. love and sex have thus become acceptable for marriage in the Christian context; today sex is not seen as result of original sin;

(Kerns, pp. 36-38)

7. the Church's teaching is not forcing limits to conjugal love, but fulfilling its obligation for Christian witness and defining its nature and guaranteeing its existence;

(McCormick, p. 72)

III. THE MEANS OF RESPONSIBLE PARENTHOOD

A. CHILD SPACING AND FAMILY SIZE:

1. not the lack of generosity but a sense of responsibility and realism imposes on a young couple the necessity of spacing pregnancies from the very beginning, even if they wish to have a large family;

(Häring, p. 6)

2. empirical research could show us where and how we are losing young people (and older ones

too) who look upon our notions of conjugal love
and natural law as neglecting realities in family
building;

(Häring, p. 7)

3. decisions on family size are to be made only by
the couple, but made according to the circumstances of the situation, the Church's general
teaching, and the inspiration of the Holy Spirit;
it must be dynamic, i.e., subject to constant re-
evaluation, and resulting from Christian prudence (whether the decision is for many or few
children) in regard to responsible parenthood.

(McCormick, p. 64)

4. the Church does not urge large families for all;

(McCormick, pp. 60-62)

5. spacing of pregnancies can have a positive and
constructive meaning in real generosity and
mutual, intimate tenderness;

(Häring, p. 11)

6. the reference to Onan (Genesis 38:9 *et seq.*) in
Casti Connubii does not prove what it wished
to prove: married couples have good and sometimes obliging reasons not to desire a pregnancy
and this is totally different from Onan, killed
because of his betrayal of wife and kinship;

(Häring, pp. 11-12)

7. a major problem recognized by almost all conference participants was the process of seminary
education in regard to marriage and sexuality;
often the real questions are not raised in the
seminary, in pastoral and moral courses; education of the clergy is viewed as a major problem and the seminary course on marriage needs

research and development; the theology of marriage needs considerable rethinking in theory (and its assumed natural law foundations) and also in practical application; this should be an integral part in the total renewal of theology; the very segregation of seminarians, often from early age, creates the ground for lack of understanding of reality; this applies to Sisters, too.

(Discussion, précis, *passim*)

B. RHYTHM:

1. defined for analytic purposes here as the systematic practice of restricting intercourse to the sterile period for the purpose of avoiding conception;

(McCormick, p. 65)

2. since effect is same (avoidance of conception), its morality is unfortunately judged morally as identical with "contraception" (use of mechanical, chemical and similar items); this is not the Catholic Church's teaching;

(McCormick, pp. 65-66)

3. how does the conjugal act fulfill the end of being procreative when rhythm is deliberately chosen? Church tradition and theologians view the sexual act as one of personal, loving communion with a specific procreative character— and to qualify objectively as an act of love, the marital embrace must be an act apt for generation, i.e., nothing is done to interfere with meeting of sperm and ovum—or just as accurately, the act must be one of total self-giving (apt for

expressing love); procreation is stressed because *a*) it more readily resists abuses of interpretation, and *b*) it faces the issue of contraception in terms of its challenge, i.e., the permanent sign of unrestricted love (procreativity) is excluded; rhythm has no such restriction;

(McCormick, pp. 66-71)

4. since rhythm is used for values other than procreation (no less essential), yet involves avoidance of children, certain conditions are morally necessary to make it morally acceptable: *a*) both parties must be willing freely; *b*) both must be able morally, without danger to sin; *c*) there must be sufficient reason, because of the problems thereby engendered for married love, e.g., tensions;

(McCormick, pp. 72-73)

5. reasons for practicing rhythm are "very wide"; Fr. John Lynch, S.J., says, "very few who bother to seek moral advice on this problem are practicing or contemplating rhythm without reason sufficient to justify the use of it . . . supposing always willingness and ability on the part of husband and wife";

(McCormick, p. 73)

6. the problem is: what happens to spontaneous, conjugal, marital love when it must be regulated by a calendar or thermometer? Spontaneity is important in sex, but Christian tradition calls for spiritual control on spontaneity, or there arises serious problems in reaching moral ends; all love must involve control;

(McCormick, pp. 73-74)

7. some argument is given that rhythm unnecessarily detracts from spontaneity; response is given, explaining that uneasiness and tension in rhythm may be attributable to poor education for married life, and possibly the decision for rhythm is selfish; there are ways of reducing tension, e.g., counselling;

(Discussion abstract; McCormick, pp. 74-75)

8. Fr. Thomas speaks of the "process of sexual relations which is procreative," thus incorporating rhythm into the classical doctrine; but if the sex acts can legitimately occur when procreation is impossible, as long as they are "in the context" of general fulfillment, what moral norms guide this? Why not also contraceptives? At least some of them? Some foods are taken when non-nutritive, but the analogy suggests that non-procreative sex acts must be of the same order as that socially and morally validated by the institution of marriage; the Lambeth Conference of 1958 abandoned "in the context" of general fulfillment and thus *a*) seems to place no moral limitation on venereal acts so long as they are mutually acceptable in Christian conscience, and *b*) refuses to assist authoritatively in the formation of the Christian conscience; actually "in the context" of general fulfillment is paradigmatic because it is both generative *and* an act of love;

(Crosson, pp. 126-128)

9. the invariant elements of love acts are that they are unitive and they are gifts; unitive of husband and wife not as objects but as persons in a special relation, i.e., union of body and soul;

it is a gift in so far as each offers freely what the other does not have; we give ourselves in the manner in which we give other things, with generosity; this is done in rhythm;

(Crosson, pp. 129-130)

10. some would say that the change in the Church's viewpoint reflected by its recognition of the morality of rhythm in the 1930's is more significant than if the Church accepted contraception today; but others point out that this is not true, because the Church had no viewpoint on rhythm until it was elucidated as a biological fact in the 1930's; historically, nonetheless, the Church in the 1930's accepted rhythm as morally justified only on rather rare occasions—then the justifying conditions were broadened—today the morally legitimate reasons for practicing rhythm are considered "in truth very wide," even for the entire life-time of the couple—this is the "revolutionary" move toward a positive approach to sexuality.

(Research, précis, *passim*)

C. THE "PILL"

1. this raises problems on which Pius XII gave a clear outline of some principles, yet left other questions open; the final decision of the Church on the latter has not been given;

(Häring, p. 18)

2. many European and some American theologians feel that an opinion will be given saying that use of these pills at the time of lactation is permissible, even if the mother is not capable of

nursing her child; reason: there seems a trend
of nature to suppress ovulation;

(Häring, p. 18)

3. arbitrary (without good and strong moral
reasons) interference with ovulation is always
bad if we use the analogy on the moral evil of
arbitrary operations;

(Häring, p. 19)

4. but if there is moral probability or certainty
that rhythm does not suffice, that full expression of conjugal love is almost necessary for
normal family life and even for the unity of the
family, then such interference (by progesterone) cannot be considered in every case arbitrary; some would consider such intervention
in very difficult cases as a lesser evil in a moral
sense, i.e., objectively sinful, but if conscience
is sincerely followed, it is on the way into the
full light; other gynecologists and some moralists consider such intervention only a lesser evil
in a physical sense;

(Häring, pp. 19-20)

5. the gap between published and unpublished
opinions on this matter by many responsible
persons, even moralists, is great;

(Häring, pp. 19-20, fn. 5)

6. a new substance in pill form, approved by the
Food and Drug Administration, gives hope for
an exact fixation and knowledge of the days of
ovulation; thus abstinence of four or five days
for rhythm can hardly be considered morally
vital for another course; this substance does not
suppress any function of nature;

(Häring, p. 20)

7. a pill could help many, but let us remember that material means and considerations must not become the center of the full Christian ideal;

(Häring, pp. 20-21)

8. direct sterilization (i.e., wherein the impossibility of conception, whether perpetual or temporary, is intended either as an end in itself or as a means to a further end) is rejected by Catholic teaching; it affects not just the good of the body as in other mutilation but also the good of the species; most "pills" tend to have this effect;

(McCormick, pp. 78-79)

9. indirect sterilization (i.e., where prevention of conception is an unintended by-product of a procedure with some other fundamental purpose) is permissible;

(McCormick, pp. 78-79)

10. some have argued that sterilization is to be rejected because it has ill-effects on interpersonal love, e.g., Joseph Fuchs, S.J., but the argument is subtle and elusive;

(McCormick, p. 80)

11. under carefully specified conditions most theologians tentatively endorse use of hormone drugs for genuinely therapeutic purposes (only incidentally sterilizing), including attempts at regularizing the cycle; endorsement is tentative because in applying the principle of "double effect" there is some question whether sterility is the means of accomplishing the other by-product effect or only a by-product thereof;

(McCormick, pp. 80-81)

12. to what extent are the following questions still "open" to moral argument? *a*) non-punitive direct sterilization (even temporary) is intrinsically immoral; *b*) contraceptive use of hormonal drugs is direct sterilization; no detailed answer is possible, but some general considerations are: *a*) a question may be "open" if it is capable of being reversed, or capable of being challenged theoretically as to conclusion or method of argument, or capable of being "nuanced," or capable of being rejected at the practical level (at what level the two questions are "open" is argued); *b*) what authority and theological status have these propositions? We can surely say that they are proposed with considerably less solemnity than the teaching on contraception; also, the rejection of contraceptive sterilization pertains to the authentic but non-infallible teaching of the Church; both propositions demand constant re-evaluation; one can frequently distinguish the conclusions from the arguments used to establish them; the effect of such propositions is, in varying degrees, a presumption of certainty which does not, however, forbid prudent investigation, discussion, publication; the theological status of the propositions seems to be that of practical certainties;

(McCormick, pp. 81-84)

13. note, however, that *a*) definitions are rarely static, and *b*) clarity of definition or principle need not imply clarity of application; refinement is possible;

(McCormick, p. 83)

D. CONTRACEPTION:

1. my view is that condom and diaphragm modify the personal act and almost invariably mislead conjugal love into selfishness; some couples assert the contrary, but even they give it up when possible, because it hurts their own dignity and respectful love;

(Häring, p. 14)

2. nor is withdrawal justified, for it spoils the personal act of giving oneself and the unity; but this withdrawal must be a complete act; in some cases the partial act may be used with self-control and in respectful expression of tenderness; this, of course, depends on conscience and sincerity;

(Häring, pp. 14-15)

3. invincible ignorance leads many people into error on this subject, though good-intentioned; this ignorance is explained by the strong public opinion favoring it and the unintegrated teaching of natural law by some of our moralists and priests;

(Häring, pp. 14-15)

4. traditional principles seem committed to the procreative character of individual conjugal acts and this is the partial basis for the contemporary authentic rejection of contraception and contraceptive sterilization;

(McCormick, p. 83)

5. Dr. Crosson's elaboration of natural law in III, B, 8 and 9 above are considered by some to have weight in proving contraception immoral; others feel that the reasoning is not conclusive.

(Crosson, pp. 125-131)

6. it can be argued that contraceptive policies do some harm to the common good of communities;

(Imbiorski, Jacobson notes)

7. the "personalist" argument on the immorality of contraceptives stresses the defective interpersonal relation established in such a setting, militating against full unity and love;

(Johann, Jacobson notes)

IV. MORAL PRINCIPLE AND SOCIAL POLICY

A. SOME BASIC ISSUES ON PUBLIC BIRTH CONTROL POLICY:

1. some premises for Catholics: *a*) no policy should be based on political expediency; *b*) the immorality of an act is not of itself a necessary or sufficient reason for prohibition by civil law (sphere of state is limited, e.g., imposition of religious beliefs); *c*) the law must maintain a prudent awareness of the public morality (law must have respect to be viable); *d*) law does exert power to lead and educate men in ordering their lives (of course, citizens may disobey unjust laws and are obliged to work for laws promoting the common good; *e*) in a pluralistic society ideological groups (religious or not) cannot expect to force their convictions or beliefs on others; *f*) yet these groups have a claim to maximum possible accommodation to pursue their ends consistent with the common good; *g*) opportunity must always be kept open for one group through zealous persuasion to convince the community that a particular ideal

should be embodied in law; *h*) in the United
States the Catholic community is the primary
force refusing governmental distribution (or
permission of others to do so) of contraceptives,
when possibly a majority find no moral problem
in such usage, or have strong belief to the contrary; some feel contraception a duty;

(Dunsford, pp. 85-89)

2. attempting to ban the *use* of contraceptives
destroys important values of individual integrity, family autonomy, and rights of privacy;
further, it is incapable of enforcement, an unjustified extension of state control over essentially private acts and breeds contempt for the
processes of law; Catholics can just disengage
from favoring such laws, but leave no doubt of
the moral evil of contraception;

(Dunsford, pp. 90-91)

3. Catholics could fulfill the important function of
dissent in a democracy by opposing *sale* and *distribution* as detrimental to the moral fiber of
the nation (likelihood of success is poor in such
dissent); this has serious disadvantages;

(Dunsford, pp. 91-92)

4. Catholics could recognize pluralism to mean
that the law acknowledge the civic right of married couples to have unimpeded access to contraceptives; this might permit Catholics to participate in the policy so that contraceptives
would be unavailable to minors and unmarried;
also this may be preferable to laws for sterilization and abortion; it could, however, give
scandal;

(Dunsford, p. 93)

B. PROBLEMS OF STATE INVOLVEMENT:

1. in England local governments have willingly
   supported family counselling centers staffed by
   Catholic doctors, which offer rhythm and social-
   spiritual guidance to all who wish to use the
   services; not much research has been done on
   this system;

   (O'Leary, discussion précis)

2. a claim can be made that the state abandons
   neutrality when it participates in a birth control
   system (i.e., it no longer has no connections
   with committed private groups, in the same
   way as the state is separated from religious institutions in the First amendment) where a substantial portion of citizens are opposed to the
   program; the defect of this position is its in-
   consistency with claims for support for private
   schools—and actually Catholics usually do not
   look for complete state neutrality; Catholics
   could approve state aid provided it is impartially and non-coercively applied;

   (Dunsford, pp. 96-97)

3. some Catholics have argued that state birth
   control involvement would mean that their tax
   dollars are being used for what they consider
   immoral purposes; actually once taxes are paid,
   they are no longer "our" tax dollars, but subject
   to general democratic decision in the use thereof;

   (Discussion précis)

4. some have proposed that Catholics support
   birth control laws publicly, provided that in
   addition to Planned Parenthood and other clinics
   there also be Catholic clinics or referral agen-

cies; there can be little legal exception to this, since all would come within coverage of public health and welfare legislation; the suggestion is that Catholic laymen run such agencies, rather than clergy; it seems desirable to have Catholics and Protestants working together on rhythm (often a common interest) and to have both working to shape public policy;

(*Ibid.*)

5. referral by publicly supported agencies of patients or clients to various agencies as indicated above involves problems, e.g., how time would be taken to determine moral acceptability to patients and with how much skill or lack of bias— a doctor or nurse persuades a client even if alternatives are offered, merely by the status of the doctor or nurse (expert status); suppose too that the client refuses limitation methods totally; suppose the state advertises the clinics; such problems may be resolvable, but they point to serious problems;

(Dunsford, pp. 98-102)

6. let us note that Catholics in Germany and elsewhere cooperate with Protestants in developing consensus and community policy; why are Catholics in this country inclined to take an exclusively separate road, largely in opposition; the problems are great and present to us now; if we wait or just continue a negative set of position, we will most probably find policies made without our participation and in spite of our moral thinking; this is contrary to our duty as citizen and as Catholic;

(Discussion précis)

7. two extreme positions may serve to clarify the problem: *a*) we may wish the state to prohibit any mention of birth control measures by public officials in welfare programs, and also no action in this regard with government support (Catholics may wish this, but it is unrealistic to most Americans and likely to fail as policy); *b*) the state may compel welfare clients to conform to state agents' recommendations (but this is totalitarian and opposed by most clear thinking citizens); some *via media* is in order and it is through discussion like this that means will be found;

(Dunsford, pp. 103-105)

8. there are many ways in which Catholics could cooperate with non-Catholics on this kind of problem; the principle of double effect, and possibly without this principle, there are morally legitimate ways; there are some important distinctions from the English experience, but morally such efforts are possible in the United States.

(Discussion précis)

This book is being published jointly
by
THE UNIVERSITY OF NOTRE DAME PRESS
and
THE CANA CONFERENCE OF CHICAGO